GENTLEMEN'S PURSUITS

A COUNTRY MISCELLANY
FOR THE DISCERNING

❃

FROM THE PAGES OF

COUNTRY LIFE

GENTLEMEN'S PURSUITS

A COUNTRY MISCELLANY FOR THE DISCERNING

FROM THE PAGES OF

COUNTRY LIFE

COUNTRY LIFE EDITOR MARK HEDGES

COMPILED AND EDITED BY SAM CARTER & KATE GATACRE
SERIES CONSULTANT JOHN GOODALL

SIMON &
SCHUSTER
ILLUSTRATED

London · New York · Sydney · Toronto · New Delhi

A CBS COMPANY

First published in Great Britain by Simon & Schuster UK Ltd, 2012
A CBS COMPANY

1 3 5 7 9 10 8 6 4 2

SIMON & SCHUSTER
ILLUSTRATED BOOKS
Simon & Schuster UK Ltd
222 Gray's Inn Road
London
WC1X 8HB

www.simonandschuster.co.uk

Simon & Schuster Australia, Sydney

Simon & Schuster India, New Delhi

Series Editor and Project Manager: Sam Carter
Series Consultant: John Goodall
Country Life Picture Library Manager: Justin Hobson
Designer: Two Associates/Richard Proctor
Literary Agent: Jonathan Conway, Mulcahy Conway Associates

A CIP catalogue record for this book is available from the British Library

ISBN 978-1-84983-766-8

Printed and bound by CPI Group (UK) Ltd, Croydon, CR0 4YY

CONTENTS

FOREWORD BY MARK HEDGES ix

1. "MANNERS MAKETH MAN" 1

Table Manners • Train Manners • "I'm Sure We All Want to Thank"
• A Seventeenth Century Entertainment • Given to Hospitality • On
Judging Fine Brandy • Re-stocking the Cellar • Shooting Lunches •
Good Wine and How to Know it • Some Considerations about Wine

2. HANDY HINTS 21

The Ideal Bonfire • Bonfire Lighters • Clothing for Winter Sports •
Camp Cooking: How to Cook a Cow's Head • A Sportsman's Tent
• To Make Boots Easy and Waterproof • A May Day Swarm • Presents
for Particular People • Our First Missile Thrower

3. THE MAN OF FASHION 35

On Smoking and Not Smoking • The Umbrella in Danger • The
Umbrella • The Fourth of June • The Tyranny of Buttons • The Tie
Collector • A New Tie • The History of the Top-Hat • The Bearded
Tide • Repressed Braces • The Modern Man's Dress • Camouflage

4. THE GREAT AND THE GOOD 53

W. G. Grace • Major-General Baden-Powell • B.-P. at Home •
The Last Despatch from Everest • Mallory • Lord Hailsham
• Marquess of Ripon • Jack London • Rudyard Kipling • Ernest
Shackleton • Captain Ball, Hero of the Air • Dr. E. A. Wilson

5. HUNTING AND HORSEMANSHIP 77

The Evolution of Hunting Costume • The Prince of Wales' First
Steeplechase • At the Grand Military • The Approach • Brighter
Elevenses • Brook Jumping • Humours of the Point-to-Point
• With the Devon and Somerset Staghounds • With the Rufford
Hunt • Hunting from London • Hunting with Foot-harriers
• Balance • Horsemanship in Rotten Row

6. SHOOTING 101

Hunting Clothes • Shooting Clothes • Shooting Notes: A Novel
Form of Pull-through • Etiquette in Covert Shooting • Wild-Fowling
in War-time • Shooting Crows with an Owl Decoy • Crocodile
Shooting • Grouse Shooting over Dogs • A Little Invention • Shooting
at Sandringham • Killing Partridges with a Tennis Racket • The
King-Emperor Shooting in Nepal • His First Heron

7. FISHING 125

The Etiquette of Fishing • The Pleasant Curiosity of Fish and Fishing
• Fishing in Montenegro • Fishing with a Glass-Bottomed Box •
Spinning Pike Baits • The Fisherman's Curse • Fishing with Dynamite
• The Prime Minister in the Western Highlands • A Fisherman's Diary
• Experiments with Fishing Gut

8. THE PLAYING FIELD 143

Our Manly Amusements • The Lawn Tennis Championships
• Curiosities of Ball-games • The Crowd and the Gate • Modern
Boxing on Exhibition • How Polo Should be Taught • The Art of
Rugby Football • The More Compleat Cricketer • The University
Boat Race

9. AVIATION AND MOTORING 161

New Cars Tested • "Driving Licence" • Dangerous Doings • Wood
is Petrol in Wartime • "The Thin End of the Wedge" • A Postcard
Adventure • "Occasional Camping by Motor Car" • Hitch and Hike
• Lighter Than Air • Soaring Flight • Air Yachting

10. SCHOOLDAYS 183

Boys on Ponies • Scouts in the Woods • Factory and Public
School Boys • The Savage and the Air-gun • What Every Schoolboy
Knows • School Cadet Corps • Gas-masks and Catapults • Three
Embryo Sportsmen

11. CURIOSITIES AND ODDITIES 197

Fitness for All • Parlour Games • A Depraved Horse • A Sportman's
Nightmare • "Arcades Ambo" • Sporting Pictures on the Human Skin
• The Hat-trick • A Little Abstinence • The Best Man • The English
Country Gentleman • The Pleasures of a Cold • A Bachelor's Wants

12. PASTIMES AND STUDY 217

Collectors' Questions • A Butterfly Hunt by the Sea • Ship Models
of Nelson's Day • The Expedition to New Guinea • A Billiard
Lover • A Book of the Day • A Casual Commentary:
A Refinement of Idleness • Lark Hunting in Wiltshire
• On Sailing • Ferreting • Yachting in London • Sand-yachting
• The Boomerang

"FEW WORDS HAVE COME TO CONVEY
SO BEAUTIFUL A MEANING AS THAT
OF 'GENTLEMAN'."

COUNTRY LIFE, 1912

FOREWORD

No other nation can match the British for their eclectic pastimes. In the field of sport we have brought the world football, rugby, cricket and lawn tennis. By way of country pastimes we have developed fox hunting, fly fishing and driven shooting. And in our desire to explore the world we have flown, sailed, driven and climbed with unmatched enthusiasm. Nor have we neglected our intellectual interests as bibliophiles, antiquarians or collectors of art, butterflies, plants, stamps and a whole host of arcane curiosities besides.

The question must be why? What has possessed the British to be so inquisitive, enthusiastic and eccentric? The answer is perhaps that we were a bunch of amateurs, a happy band of people who could freely pursue their hobbies. By definition, a gentleman is a landowner, and consequently had a great interest in improving things: his land, his livestock and his hobbies. Add to the recipe the empire, which made the British outward looking, and you have cooked up a group of people who had the time, means and interest to change the world.

Since its first publication in 1897 during the reign of Queen Victoria, *Country Life* has recorded the full and bewildering variety of activities, enthusiasms and sports at which a British gentleman might proudly excel. Brought together here is a selection of short articles from past issues of the magazine on this theme, from shooting to after-dinner speaking and from beekeeping to ferreting.

Here additionally are insights into the very qualities that make a gentleman, his manners, possessions, tastes and even some of his secrets (discover the truth here about aristocratic tattoos). There are pieces, moreover, on some of the figures who have set the standards of amateur excellence: W. G. Grace, Baden-Powell, Mallory, Kipling and Shackleton.

Above and beyond all this are some are practical tips on bonfires, throwing boomerangs and ways in which poetry can help you approach a fence in the hunting field. Clearly this is a book that no gentleman can afford to be without.

Oscar Wilde once described: 'The English country gentleman galloping after a fox – the unspeakable in full pursuit of the uneatable', but he failed to recognise the genius of the idea in the first place. This book celebrates what he missed.

MARK HEDGES

EDITOR OF COUNTRY LIFE

MAY 2012

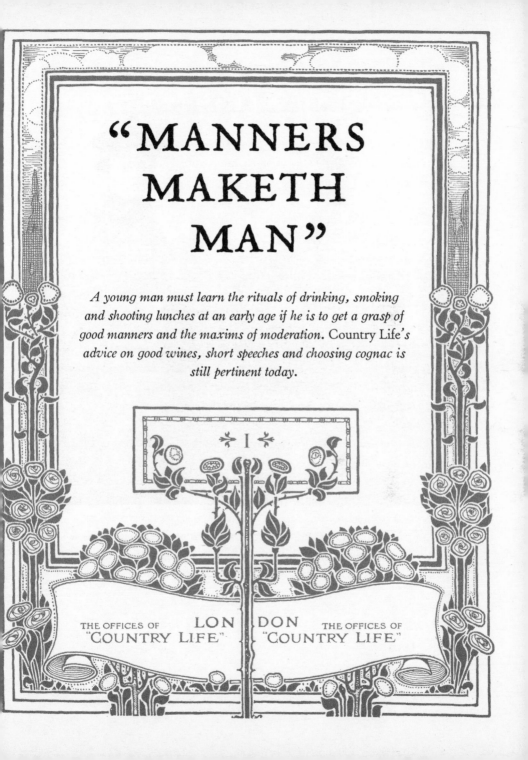

"MANNERS MAKETH MAN"

A young man must learn the rituals of drinking, smoking and shooting lunches at an early age if he is to get a grasp of good manners and the maxims of moderation. Country Life's advice on good wines, short speeches and choosing cognac is still pertinent today.

❋ I ❋

THE OFFICES OF "COUNTRY LIFE" LONDON THE OFFICES OF "COUNTRY LIFE"

JUNE 19ᵀᴴ, 1942

TABLE MANNERS

Lord Woolton, the minister for food during World War II, was famous for his useful advice on austerity measures, though evidently not everyone found it easy to cut down on bread and butter.

FEW MEN CAN say more truly of us than can Lord Woolton: "I know their tricks and their manners," and now he wants us to alter our bread-and-butter manners. We must refrain from tearing open our roll or hastily breaking our toast, thus wasting crumbs; we must eat it tidily. We must not prepare bread and butter on a lavish scale and pile it on a plate, but only cut it bit by bit as it is wanted. We must not put a piece of butter or a spoonful of jam on to our plate, making a rough and perhaps prodigal estimate of our needs. No, we must spread the precious stuff directly from the dish or the pot on to our piece of bread.

"WE CANNOT SPREAD IT TOO THICK FOR VERY SHAME"

This is clearly a good "austerity" plan, for we cannot spread it too thick for very shame, whereas if we in our old bad way have made an overestimate we may always hope for a last unctuous mouthful or two in order not to cut any more bread. Some may suffer severely, and in particular he who has been defined as a gentleman because he always uses the butter-knife even when alone. A painful alternative is now before him; he must either spread his butter with the butter-knife or cut the butter with his ordinary one.

SEPTEMBER 4TH, 1942

TRAIN MANNERS

IN SO FAR as politeness consists of consideration for others the war has generally made for more rather than less of it. It has taught us that unselfishness consists largely, in Emerson's words, of making a number of "petty sacrifices," and we make them with a tolerably good grace. But letters to various newspapers have lately suggested that our train manners are not perfect. The smoker who was once kept rigidly within bounds has waxed arrogant with the greater licence allowed him. He can indulge anywhere but in a non-smoking carriage, and yet when he gets into one he is apt to blackmail the other occupants by asking: "Do you mind my smoking?" He asks the question, moreover, in a tone demanding but one reply. If he talked in the language of the Latin grammar he would preface his question with "*Num*," expecting the answer "No."

> "IF HE TALKED IN THE LANGUAGE OF THE LATIN GRAMMAR HE WOULD PREFACE HIS QUESTION WITH '*NUM*'"

Another complaint is against those in first-class carriages. Those who take first-class tickets have often a legitimate grievance in that their seats are occupied by third-class ticketholders. Yet when they have a seat they are rather grudging in making room for others. Admittedly three aside spells comfort and four aside discomfort. The man with a seat cannot be like the good Samaritan with an umbrella who summons two friends and so remains dry in the middle while they both get wet. Nevertheless, to offer to make room for one standing wearily in the corridor is a piece of ordinary decent manners that should be made without a request.

MAY 26ᵀᴴ, 1928

"I'M SURE WE ALL WANT TO THANK"

The tedium of listening to long speeches might be relieved if the suggestions in this article gained greater currency.

CAN NONE OF you do anything to make speech-making – both the speaking and the listening – easier for us of the English countryside? The number of our occasions for meeting and speaking seems to be growing ever greater, but at present we do not appear to get much beyond the stage where half a dozen crippled sentences, beginning with "I'm sure we all want to thank," represent our highest achievement.

More than half our troubles of today can be dated back to that presumptuous experiment made at Babel. When the people sought to take misguided advantage of the fact that they could by then speak, all together, in one language.

Men of the English countryside do not, in any narrow sense, require to be taught how to speak; what we need is to be told what to say. All of you, the clever speakers, must come to the aid of our crippled sentences individually, you must each, individually and by your personal example, do your best to make those crippled speeches of ours strong – and happy.

The rough-and-ready rules which are all you have given us up to the present – these are no longer enough for our need. "Stand up, speak up, shut up"; "Have something to say, say it, sit down".

It seems to us of the countryside that speeches are an individual, a personal, matter, because we know how greatly we have been affected by the personalities of you, the good speakers, from whom we have learned the little we know of speechmaking.

If you who are good enough to come to speak to us will only be sincere with us – and sympathetic in the fullest sense and having a sound knowledge of your subject – we shall be most grateful to you, and shall learn from you, quite rapidly, how to conduct our business of the English countryside. In short, we shall all want to thank you – when you have taught us how to do so.—CRASCREDO

DECEMBER 24TH, 1927

A SEVENTEENTH CENTURY ENTERTAINMENT

The English kitchen may have come in for some trenchant criticism in more recent times, but clearly there was a flair for the dramatic during the dinners of the seventeenth century.

TO THE EDITOR OF "COUNTRY LIFE."

SIR,—I doubt whether any of your readers would be sufficiently enterprising – I might say courageous – to carry out the suggestions for the amusement of guests made by Robert May in his *Whole Body of Cookery Dissected*, a volume published in 1661 and now rather scarce. Here is one of his most ingenious schemes: As a centrepiece there was "a stag of coarse paste with an arrow in the side of him and his body filled with wine," which was surrounded by salt in which were stuck egg-shells filled with rose-water. "At one side of the charger wherein is the Stag is placed a Pye in which there be some live Frogs, and at the other, one with live birds, the crusts of both pies being decorated with gilt bay leaves. All being placed upon the table order it so that some of the Ladies may be persuaded to pluck the arrow out of the Stag, then will the wine follow as blood running out of a wound... By this time you may suppose they will desire to see what is in the Pye, where first lifting the lid off one out skip the Frogs which makes the Ladies to skip and skreek; next after the other Pye when come out the Birds which, by a natural instinct flying at the Light, will put out the candles so that the flying Birds and

> "THEN WILL THE WINE FOLLOW AS BLOOD RUNNING OUT OF A WOUND"

> "OUT SKIP THE FROGS WHICH MAKES THE LADIES TO SKIP AND SKREEK"

the skipping Frogs, the one above, the other beneath, will cause much delight and pleasure to the Company."

Furthermore, besides the stag and the pies and their contents, toy cannon in pasteboard ships were to be fired on the table, and the ladies, "to sweeten the stink of the powder," were to take the eggshells of rosewater and throw them at each other! It must have been a jocund scene!—R. E. HEAD

SEPTEMBER 29TH, 1928

GIVEN TO HOSPITALITY

Sometimes it is a blessing when things do not go according to plan –
accepting a night of hospitality sounds far more delightful than motoring
through the night. Unfortunately, the writer fails to list the other fifty-six
things a man should do in his lifetime.

NOW THAT THERE is more liveliness in country life – more
parties of every kind being given than ever before – it is time
to explode this monstrous notion that anybody can be kind
and hospitable if they've only got the money.

In the country, at any rate, party-giving has still all that personal
element of kindness about it which may have been lost at some of the
parties given in our towns. "You produce the guest – we do all the rest"
– that is a slogan of the greater London
catering firms, charmingly seeking to sustain
a fiction that London hostesses do produce
their own guests. London hostesses have for
long been aware that their guests produce
each other, and to an extent which is only
sometimes alarming.

"THAT IS AMONG
THE FIFTY-SEVEN
THINGS WHICH
EVERY MAN
SHOULD DO ONCE
IN HIS LIFETIME"

I will tell you of the house of So-and-
So. We came to that house late of a summer's
evening, on a sudden decision, having intended to go on motoring all
through the night. That is among the fifty-seven things which every man
should do once in his lifetime. I do not mean that he should go to a house
unbidden. I mean that he should go motoring all through the night on
one night of his life. Or, rather, he should do it twice: once he should do
it at speed – swooping through the valleys, flying up the hills, kicking
the miles behind him in the darkness as a galloping horse kicks back at a
bank which he has flown in one leap. It will be all to the good if he comes

through the storm that night, and if at some stage of that journey there should be lightnings and thunder, great splashings and torrent of rain.

But first came the butler. That sort of butler should be written with a capital B (for Blessed). At dinner in a long, low room with candles among the glass and silver, racing cups and pictures, and a *jaune clair* dessert service painted by Provost, there was quiet talk about this and that.

And long after dinner, when a guest with any manners at all would have got into his car without wobbling – with, I mean, a firmness of purpose, determined not to impose upon hospitality any longer – why, then, we wobbled. Or, rather, we scarcely had to wobble. It just came to be understood, at about eleven o'clock, that we were staying the night.

Then God preserve the spirit of So and of So, his wife – a very gentle couple, who gave to their parties what was *meant* for mankind.— CRASCREDO

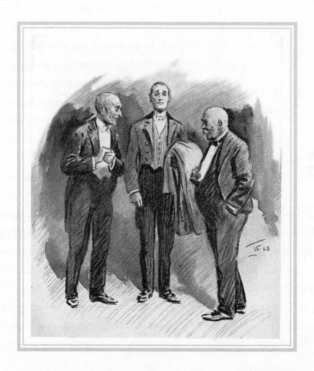

ON JUDGING FINE BRANDY

IT IS THE ambition of every man of taste to be a judge of fine brandy. He knows already a great deal – he must know it if he is a man of taste – about certain fine wines. And he knows that a good many so-called wines he is asked to drink bear the same relation to a Lafite '99, shall we say, as *Crème de Menthe* does to a *Grande Champagne* of '48. But the sugary fluids which appeal to the ladies of his house are not in question. He realises already that among the brandies, actual and supposed, which he is asked to drink, some are not brandy, some are faked brandy, many are bad brandy, a few are good brandy, and fewer still are that precious nectar which he longs to identify as a Grande Champagne of a good year. Let us consider what are the factors involved in making himself an expert in this matter.

> "IT IS THE AMBITION OF EVERY MAN OF TASTE TO BE A JUDGE OF FINE BRANDY"

To begin with, he knows that any good and unfaked brandy must have somewhere about it a flavour which identifies it with the grape. It is true enough that the wines grown in France, whether in the Charente for the production of Cognac or farther south where Armagnac is produced, have this at least in common, that they are completely undrinkable to the foreigner, harsh and bitter as the flintiest that ever called itself Chablis. But this delightful paradox that the worst wine – from a wine drinker's point of view – makes the best brandy, does not invalidate the proposition that there, at the back of every really fine brandy, is the subtlest essence of the grape. As soon as one begins to swallow a faked brandy the flavour has gone, but with a fine brandy it lingers on the palate with a taste and smell faintly reminiscent of household bread.

The man of taste will drink his brandy from a far smaller glass – not one of those glass thimbles from which his daughter sips her *noyau* or maraschino, but a good round glass bulging downward from the rim and with a wide enough mouth for the nose and the palate to be used at the same time.

The glass must, therefore, be small enough for the hand to clasp and thin enough for the hand's warmth to penetrate.

When the bouquet has been enjoyed to the full, take a sip and let it roll round the tongue, breathing down the nose the while.

A WINE AUCTION ABOUT 1820.

AUGUST 21ST, 1926

RE-STOCKING THE CELLAR

To the Editor of "Country Life."

Sir,—The fall in the French exchange gives us a splendid opportunity of re-stocking our war-depleted cellars by purchasing really sound Bordeaux and Burgundies at less than pre-war prices. Cheap claret costs a negligible sum in France today, and for a round ten shillings a dozen the visitor can secure really good, sound wines already bottled. Far the best way to secure cheap wine is to buy a small cask of sound Médoc or Burgundy and ship it to England, where it can be bottled at any local wine merchant's. Anyone with fairly large cellarage in a country house would be well advised to consider a special trip to France for the purpose of laying the foundations of a really good cellar of wine.

> "ANYONE WITH FAIRLY LARGE CELLARAGE IN A COUNTRY HOUSE WOULD BE WELL ADVISED TO CONSIDER A SPECIAL TRIP TO FRANCE"

The private buyer who relies on his own palate, and who deals with good French firms, need have little fear that his experiment will turn out badly. Above all, there is virtue in experiment and it is to the interest of both countries that wine drinking should not be allowed to fall into a decline because English retailers still wish to preserve the ridiculous level of war prices.—JEROBOAM

AUGUST 7TH, 1920

SHOOTING LUNCHES

SPECIALISED APPARATUS FOR the serving of shooting lunches is in scarce supply, wicker for baskets, enamelled iron ware, and glass – to name only a few details and not to mention labour and other obstacles which stand in the way of routine production. These and other details I have culled in the course of a tour among our leading specialists.

How to Pack Bread and Sandwiches
The staff of life is best carried in a sack, or preferably a specially made canvas bag. This suggestion is very practical, for bread, to retain its crispness, must not be confined in any sort of closed receptacle. There must be free evaporation at the surface, otherwise the moisture escaping

from the middle will render the crust sodden. This question of moisture is really worth considering scientifically, for it prevents the packing of cake and biscuits in the same box. They must not be stored in company, since one is boxed to keep it moist, the other to maintain its dryness.

Hot Dishes for Chilly Days

Hot boxes are, perhaps, the most noteworthy aid to a shooting lunch. Outside they are a sort of plainly varnished packing case, larger than a hat-box, smaller perhaps than a kettle-drum. The inside view discloses a sort of tin bucket closely packed around with felt. Inside the bucket are three removable tins, one large and two smaller ones, the first holding meat, the others vegetables.

"THE STAFF OF LIFE IS BEST CARRIED IN A SACK, OR PREFERABLY A SPECIALLY MADE CANVAS BAG"

Cold Dishes

Over-elaboration of the menu is always to be avoided, therefore, if ideas bristle in seeming excess of number when the subject is considered theoretically, the excuse, or rather the explanation, must be that you do not in practice crowd all your ideas into one menu. Jam tarts and cheesecakes, by the way, are the great stand-by of a shooting meal. Very often they follow "something hot," their merit being that they involve no extra plate or special cutlery for serving.

Shooting is a great sport, nobody expects to make it a cheap one, but at the finish its success largely depends on the untiring conscientiousness of the beaters. To see that they have a good lunch is but an item in the total of organisation which every shooting day involves, but it is an item which repays continuous attention. Good news of this sort has a wide circulation.—Shot

JUNE 11TH, 1921

GOOD WINE AND HOW TO KNOW IT

HERE IS A hazardous title. The maxims to be observed would be heartily applauded if applied to business or sport. Begin early; persevere; omit no opportunity of improving your knowledge and taste. What wholesome advice is this for the boy entering an office or ambitious of emulating the fame of Dr. Grace or James Baird but —

> "WHEN A YOUNG MAN COMES OF AGE IS A VERY GOOD TIME TO BEGIN"

applied to wine? At the best they are sure to be marked with a large note of interrogation or described as milestones on the road to ruin. But that is to misunderstand. Early is a comparative term. Childhood, when the foundations of constitution are being laid, ought to be kept free of two things – drink and tobacco. I once knew a patriotic small farmer who insisted on giving beer to each of his children the day after it was weaned; and there used to pass our way a woman tramp who gave her children gin in order to keep them small and thin. It must not be thought that there is any wish to bring back customs like these. When a young man comes of age is a very good time to begin, so that he may have obtained an understanding of the ritual of drinking before he reaches thirty. It is a ritual far more carefully observed by the moderate than the immoderate.

FOR THE CONNOISSEUR

APRIL 7TH, 1928

SOME CONSIDERATIONS ABOUT WINE

Some excellent advice on choosing the right wine for each dish, and leaving the magnums to the magnates.

IT IS EXTRAORDINARY how many English people live (and die none the later) under the superstition that it is wrong to "mix your drinks." The French, who bestow more intelligent care on the digestion than any other people in Europe, always serve a succession of wines with a meal of any pretensions. This is not only for better enjoyment of their liquor – though serious drinkers will say that Brillat-Savarin is right, and that the palate is cloyed by any wine after the third glass of it, so that change is prescribed for valiant persons. But even those who use wine in the most studious moderation recognise the harmony or the discord between certain wines and certain viands. Above all, in the broadest generalisation, red wine does not go well with fish – though connoisseurs make an exception for red mullet among fishes, and for Beaujolais among red wines.

I illustrate from the proceedings of the patron at the Hôtel de la Couronne in Rouen – which was an inn before the burning of Jeanne d'Arc; he gave us two half-bottles, so as to have white wine with our *sole normande*. Here again we ran counter to another widespread English superstition, which teaches that good wine is not to be had in half-bottles. Our host, at all events, putting his best foot foremost, was in no way afraid to discredit his house by producing his chablis and his *Châteauneuf du Pape* in pints.

Magnates, of course, can get what they want by paying for it, and in magnums if they choose. But I address these remarks to the humble people, like myself, for whom one of the most amusing adventures is the hunt for something that is good to drink and not beyond their means.— STEPHEN GWYNN

HANDY
HINTS

*Mostly practical, but occasionally whimsical,
Country Life's tips on camping, kit and cooking a
cow's head are essential for the gentleman who enjoys
the great outdoors.*

✦ II ✦

THE OFFICES OF   LONDON   THE OFFICES OF
"COUNTRY LIFE"   "COUNTRY LIFE"

THE IDEAL BONFIRE

*Lighting a fire is one of man's most primitive skills – here is a rather
sophisticated version of putting a flame to the garden rubbish.*

To the Editor of "Country Life."

Sir,—In every garden there is a heap of slowly decaying rubbish.
Eventually all this vegetable matter would be converted into an elemental
state, but with much of the material, such as the clippings from evergreen
hedges, the process of decomposition would take years to complete. Yet,
all the time, there are present in this rubbish valuable plant foods which,
in a well ordered garden should find their way back to the soil. The quick
way to recover much of this useful matter is to make a bonfire of the
stuff and then dig the ashes into the ground. It is easy to burn up almost
anything in a short while and with a very small amount of smoke. Here is

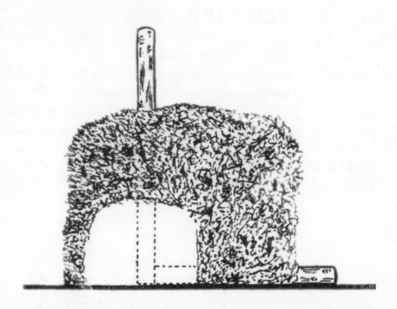

the way to start the ideal bonfire. Get two wooden stakes, one of which is placed upright in the ground and the other is laid at the foot in horizontal fashion. These stakes might be 3 ft. or 4 ft. long and should be several inches in diameter. Around the stakes heap the rubbish to be burned in the manner shown in the sketch.

Take especial care to press the material down very firmly so that a compact mass is secured. When the pile is complete, pull away the stakes. There will then be an air channel right from the heart of the mass which will act just like a chimney. To start the fire push lighted paper into the lower hole and at once the flames draw away with a roaring noise. From thenceforward the fire will burn steadily until everything is consumed.—S. LEONARD BASTIN

FEBRUARY 9ᵀᴴ, 1929
BONFIRE LIGHTERS

TO THE EDITOR OF "COUNTRY LIFE."

SIR,—Some of your readers, who are puzzled as to the disposal of the discarded outer covers of motor tyres, may be interested to hear that they form the best possible bonfire lighters. The covers should be cut through into lengths of 6 ins. to 9 ins. Two or three of these sections placed on a small quantity of straw or similar material will start a bonfire, which would otherwise necessitate laborious preparation.—G. E. BURNETT-STUART

JANUARY 10TH, 1914

CLOTHING FOR WINTER SPORTS

The early days of skiing were undoubtedly hindered by a costume of breeches and puttees. A reader suggests a more practical mode of dressing for winter sports.

To the Editor of " Country Life."

SIR,—I read with interest your articles on clothing for skiing in the Alps, but was surprised to find that most of your correspondents seem to favour breeches or knickerbockers with puttees.

The chief thing in choosing a skiing outfit is to see that the cloth of the suit, the outer covering of gauntlets, the cap, etc. – in short, the outside of everything – is perfectly smooth. The slightest hairiness in the texture gives the snow a chance to stick, and this snow then melts, owing to the body warmth, and sinks slowly through and into the cloth. I was once or twice caught in a snowstorm with a friend who wore a "homespun" suit. The result was, when we got under shelter, he was soaked through and I

> "I WAS SURPRISED TO FIND THAT MOST OF YOUR CORRESPONDENTS SEEM TO FAVOUR BREECHES OR KNICKERBOCKERS..."

was fairly dry, as I was able to brush the adhered snow off easily. Harris tweeds and homespuns are perfect for most sporting purposes, but for sports that have to do with snow, such as skiing, tobogganing, bobbing, etc., they are not advisable – especially for skiing. With apologies for having trespassed on your valuable space.—W. G. EHRENBACH

JULY 3ʳᵈ, 1915

CAMP COOKING: HOW TO COOK A COW'S HEAD

An easy meal if you have a cow to hand and have set up camp for the night.

To the Editor of "Country Life."

Sir,—Perhaps the following recipe, which was retailed to me by an ex-cowboy, may be useful to the many mess cooks who have to cook in the open for the soldiers: Butcher the cow, hang up all parts but the head for future use. The sooner the meat is cooked the tenderer it will be. Take a "gunny" sack, lard it with clay, inside it place the head, unskinned, but saw off the horns. Dig a square or round hole from 18 in. to 2 ft. deep; at the bottom place hot ashes of pinion or cedar about 6 in. deep. On this layer place the sack with the head tied inside so that the

> "THOSE IN THE 'KNOW' MAKE FOR THE BRAIN AND THE TONGUE"

head be almost level with the ground, but leaving a small space, which fill up with another layer of hot ashes. On top of this build a fire which will last through the night. Return to your tent, roll yourself in your blankets and wait for dawn. Awake, get your coffee ready, place the head in a "skillet" lid, draw around with your tin plates and attack. Those in the "know" make for the brain and the tongue.—C. H. M. Johnstone

A SPORTSMAN'S TENT

TO THE EDITOR OF "COUNTRY LIFE."

SIR,—I send you a photograph from Burma that may interest you. This is a Survey umbrella tent. It is the best tent imaginable for a sportsman. It is 7 ft. in height, so that there is no stooping, and has a diameter of 12 ft. It can be pitched on a hillside, and is only one coolie's load. Moreover, it is wind-proof. This one has been in Tibet, where the wind can be dreadful, and in unexplored Africa.

> "IT IS THE BEST TENT IMAGINABLE FOR A SPORTSMAN"

I hope it may interest big-game hunters. If any of them want one, they can get it from the Elgin Mills Company of Cawnpore.—T. R. LIVESEY

OCTOBER 3ᴿᴰ, 1914

TO MAKE BOOTS EASY AND WATERPROOF

To the Editor of "Country Life."

SIR,—Would you please inform me of a good recipe for softening the leather of boots and at the same time waterproofing it? The recipe, if possible, must be of easy application, easily made and not expensive or injurious in the leather. I want it for boots to be used on the march.—G. R. J.

"I WANT IT FOR BOOTS TO BE USED ON THE MARCH"

[Warm the boots thoroughly through, then rub in Russian tallow or soak the boots in castor oil. This will make them thoroughly pliable; and for waterproofing there is nothing to beat dubbin.—Ed]

MAY 10TH, 1913

A MAY DAY SWARM

To the Editor of "Country Life."

Sir,—There is a quaint old rhyme, known to most bee-masters, which runs as follows:

> A swarm in May
> Is worth a load of hay;
> A swarm in June,
> A silver spoon.
> But a swarm in July
> Is not worth a fly.

I cannot be certain that the May Day swarm represented in the accompanying photograph will bring me in the value of "a load of hay," but, judging by the size of the colony, I think there is every chance of it doing so. It is one of the finest swarms I have taken in my Riviera garden. The queen and her followers settled not more than three yards from the apiary, and on a wild plum tree which, I have noticed, has been chosen year after year by my bees when swarming. *"Aussi inoffensives qu'une nuée de libellules ou de phalènes,"* as Maeterlinck says, they allowed me to place them in their new home; and as I provided them with four frames of empty comb, the queen began her work at once.

"A SWARM IN MAY IS WORTH A LOAD OF HAY"

On the following day the workers went collecting honey among the orange blossom. Trusting that this little item will interest your readers.— Frederic Lees La Buissonniere, Cagnes, AM, France

DECEMBER 12TH, 1931

PRESENTS FOR PARTICULAR PEOPLE

Practical presents are not always what is wanted – evidently the frivolous is often met with more enthusiasm.

OST OF US are fortunate in having at least one friend with an unerring skill in the choice of presents. Though there are people born with this capacity the art is not difficult to acquire, even though one may not quite reach the supreme height of having "the Kingdom of Heaven within, and a sense of humour without" with which these particular friends are inspired. Do not, in any case, let us forget that surprise is as important as fitness where presents are concerned; it is easy to avoid the obvious and score a success with a perfectly commonplace article. A really superfine bath sponge may make a man happy who has few personal wants. A gift has an added charm if it flatters one's self-importance; a "man's" dressing case, complete with

razor, pleases the lad who must wait some time to use it; and a cocktail cabinet for country cousins may give more satisfaction than the tin-lined weeding basket with secateurs and trowel that at the first glance seemed a more appropriate gift.

A succession of warm shawls, hot water bottles or fur-lined slippers gives greater price, by sheer force of contrast, to your gay and glittering trifle, in the eyes of a septuagenarian great-aunt. On the other hand, uncles, aunts, godfathers and godmothers (to whom presents for the young are a recurrent problem) may save the annual cogitation over Christmas gifts by the selection of one that forms part of a series. A pearl necklace is a princely gift in itself, and happy is he that gives and she that receives it. But even though we cannot all present all our friends with ropes of pearls every year, we

"SURPRISE IS AS
IMPORTANT AS
FITNESS WHERE
PRESENTS ARE
CONCERNED"

need not forget that we can still give a pearl every year to form ultimately a necklace, or a volume of the works of some standard author, and that these things become a source of great satisfaction as time goes on, and result in a possession that is really valuable and lasts a lifetime.

OUR FIRST MISSILE THROWER

*Catapults are not only for the younger generation, as, in combination with
acorns, they have their uses as a method of chastising dogs. Beware that
you are not accused of smashing streetlights, however.*

SOME YEARS AGO I wrote an article on catapults, illustrating it
with several of the examples in my collection; and, judging by
the response in the way of correspondence, the subject proved
of greater interest than many a more serious contribution on gunnery
matters. Apart from the reminiscences of boyhood escapades in days
long before the air-gun, details were supplied by grown-up users of
this elementary form of projectile thrower.
For instance, an explorer wrote from Africa
saying that his catapult proved of daily
service for the collection of specimens. In the
management of dogs they also have their use,
since no better corrective of the tendency to
wander from the orthodox position at heel
is available than one of these instruments,
a supply of acorns or such like serving as
pellets. The punishment inflicted is no more
severe than a cut with the whip, but is more
effective, since it imparts the impression that
control can be exercised across a dividing space. The particular sample,
here illustrated in two stages of production, has interesting associations.

"BOYS ARE
USUALLY
SATISFIED WITH
A VERY ROUGH
RESULT, BUT TRUE
ARTISTRY AIMS
AT A SOMEWHAT
HIGHER
STANDARD"

Some time ago I was morally instrumental in the loss of a certain
naturalist's treasured specimen. Espying in the woods one day what
seemed to be a nicely grown fork, I removed it from the branch and took
it home with a view to making partial amends for the above-mentioned
tragedy – for such it undoubtedly was. Nearly all forks in the raw need

careful setting before they can be allowed to dry. Mere tying of the prongs with string usually produces a lop-sided result, the better plan being to screw them down on a board with metal straps in the manner shown. After a few days in the hot-air closet they can be removed for trimming and general fashioning into finished shape, the last-named stage being also shown. Boys are usually satisfied with a very rough result, but true artistry aims at a somewhat higher standard. Elderly folk must be very cautious should they permit themselves to revert to earlier joys by way of using one of these implements, for, if indulging in a public place, they are liable to be rudely accosted and accused of being the long-sought fiend whose secret pleasure is the breaking of roadside lamps; but, this handicap apart, there is decided pleasure in testing what remains of one's earlier skill.—MAX BAKER

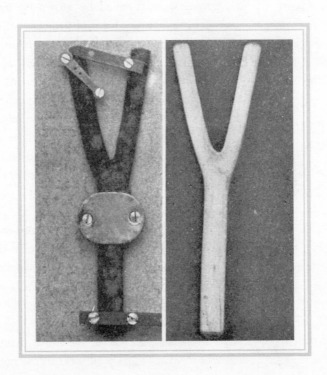

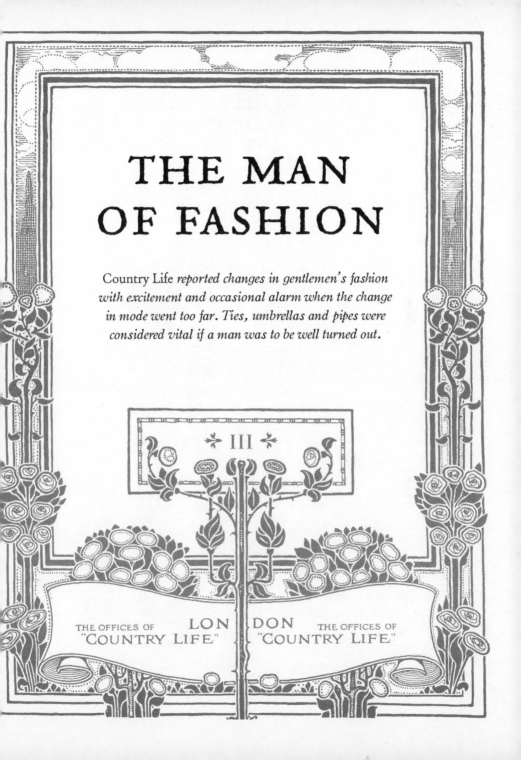

THE MAN
OF FASHION

Country Life *reported changes in gentlemen's fashion
with excitement and occasional alarm when the change
in mode went too far. Ties, umbrellas and pipes were
considered vital if a man was to be well turned out.*

✦ III ✦

THE OFFICES OF   LONDON   THE OFFICES OF
"COUNTRY LIFE"   "COUNTRY LIFE"

ON SMOKING AND
NOT SMOKING

Here's how to tell a man by his pipe.

THE FASHIONS OF smoking are, naturally enough, in some measure moulded by the times and the climate in which we live. The country gentleman of Georgian days could give his time to it. By day he rode to hounds, and in the evening what better than to call for his long clay pipe and puff away in contentment by the cheerful warmth of an open fire? In the hustle of modern life the clay pipe has gone, and is only to be seen, very much shortened, in the mouths of navvies, or perverted to more frivolous uses between the lips of children. In the East, where men take their pleasures sedately, the hookah still finds favour.

> "IN THE EAST, WHERE MEN TAKE THEIR PLEASURES SEDATELY, THE HOOKAH STILL FINDS FAVOUR"

It is not only of a period or of a nation that the manner of smoking is a characteristic. It distinguishes the individual. Some say you can tell a man by his shoes, others by his hat; but, to my mind, there is much more to be learnt from the way in which he smokes. Consider the pipe first of all, for it is the medium most expressive in itself, most protean in its shapes, and most cherished by its devotees. Do we not unconsciously associate that heavy "bulldog" pipe, with

a large bowl and tremendous curve to its mouthpiece, with the deliberate, good-natured, reasonable sort of fellow? And the man who fingers lovingly a little round bowl at the end of the long stem of a churchwarden: he is surely one who delights in fine arguments and philosophic niceties expounded from the depth of a comfortable armchair. Then there are all manner of strange pipes, carved to queer shapes – the rugged Algerian briar, the musical-looking calabash, or that richly coloured Italian *bruyere* now so much the fashion, with any of which the Englishman may gratify his passion for individualism. Indeed, it is only meet and proper that a pipe should be something more than a generator of fumes to a man. We ought to make an art of our pleasures. A large portion of any pleasure is the specious atmosphere we contrive to put around it – illusions, if you will; but what is life without them? To smoke any old tobacco in any old pipe is but a shadow of the real art.

AUGUST 28ᵀᴴ, 1942

THE UMBRELLA IN DANGER

O NE BY ONE "our social comforts drop away" the latest threat to them is that we shall not be able to get our umbrellas re-covered, unless we can find an artist licensed to do it. Let us hope that such licences will be generously distributed, or our old and trusty friend may yet be laughed at by rude street boys, as was the first umbrella in Cranford, as "a stick in petticoats," and torn, scant ones at that.

Englishmen are a race of umbrella-carriers. We feel safe beneath its shadow as we should in a suit of armour. The late Mr. R. H. Macaulay used to tell a pleasant story in illustration. When he was a boy at Eton he and J. K. S. had one day been practising with a 16 lb. weight and finally heaved it on to the top of a certain arch leading into the Playing Fields, where it remained insecurely poised. At that moment

> "ENGLISHMEN ARE A RACE OF UMBRELLA-CARRIERS"

there appeared the Provost, to whom, with some embarrassment, they explained the danger. He thanked them gravely, put up his umbrella and walked under the arch. If these, our natural protectors, are by stern decree taken from us we shall feel sadly naked. The stealing of umbrellas may become as common a crime as the stealing of bicycles. Only the wicked will remain dry, because on a rainy day, as we know from a familiar poem: 'The unjust's got the just's umbrella.'

FEBRUARY 27TH, 1937

THE UMBRELLA

To the Editor of "Country Life."

Sir,—Probably because I live in the FitzGerald district, the article on umbrellas in your issue of February 13th reminded me of the following story.

Edward FitzGerald, with his manservant, on one occasion travelled to London by train. On arrival at Liverpool Street it was found that FitzGerald's umbrella had been forgotten. A return ticket was bought, and while Edward FitzGerald sat on the platform and waited, the manservant returned to Woodbridge for the umbrella.—Edith Hurry

"WHILE EDWARD FITZGERALD SAT ON THE PLATFORM AND WAITED, THE MANSERVANT RETURNED TO WOODBRIDGE FOR THE UMBRELLA"

JUNE 11TH, 1932

THE FOURTH OF JUNE

THOUGH UNCERTAINTY PREVAILED almost to the last moment as to whether the flooded condition of the river would permit the full time-honoured programme of the Procession of Boats at Eton on the Fourth, spectators of the fireworks were not entirely disappointed. The crews did not "toss their oars" and come drifting down stream. But, at the traditional moment, the boats did pull upstream with the ruddy glow illuminating white ducks and festive hats. This year, indeed, members of the boats were more than usually the cynosure of ladies' eyes owing to the fashionable style of their headgear, and in the neighbourhood of the Brocas several exchanges of the kind associated with Hampstead Heath were effected. The coxes, though always resplendent in their guise of Captains of the Pinafore, were, perhaps, a little out shadowed this year as a result of the partiality of ladies for the gents' boater.

NOVEMBER 22ND, 1946

THE TYRANNY OF BUTTONS

SHERLOCK HOLMES ONCE pointed out that Watson had seen but had not observed, since, often as he had ascended to the well-known room in Baker Street, he did not know the number of the steps. Most men are in a similar state of ignorance as to the number of buttons which they must every morning insert into the appropriate buttonholes. A writer of a letter to *The Times* has lately obeyed Holmes's precept and counted his buttons, with the surprising result that there were no fewer than twenty-nine of them to be tackled. He enviously pointed out that his daughter had only four buttons in all and there is here a grave inequality of labour. The zip fastener provides one obvious remedy. Men do use it on the jackets in which they play golf and do other outdoor things, but the principle might be widely extended.

> "MOST MEN ARE IN A SIMILAR STATE OF IGNORANCE AS TO THE NUMBER OF BUTTONS WHICH THEY MUST EVERY MORNING INSERT INTO THE APPROPRIATE BUTTONHOLES"

FEBRUARY 4ᵀᴴ, 1939

THE TIE COLLECTOR

I T WAS STATED in the newspapers not long since that a debating society would discuss the motion "That this house detests the old school tie." I imagine that the words referred to the implications of the tie rather than to the thing itself, and that some fiery young person was going to thunder against public schools and snobbishness and old gentlemen who never grew up and that sort

"A POOR, MUTE PIECE OF SILK" of thing. If so, I have not the slightest desire to break a lance with him; but if he meant to attack a poor, mute piece of silk that cannot defend itself then I must mildly protest, because a tie is the one human garment in which I take an interest. I may even, in a very humble way, call myself a collector. Perhaps I ought rather to say that I was a collector, because the other day I was induced – or compelled – to throw away some of the rarest and, if the truth be known, the dirtiest of my treasures. Without any warning, a tidal wave of spring cleaning swept through my house.

No collector who is worthy the name would, I imagine, acquire ties that he could not wear in the open light of day. That would be like buying a stolen Old Master, only to peep at it now and then behind locked doors. On the other hand, he does find it entertaining to possess ties of which no one would suspect him.

One of my last Christmas presents was a truly elegant and quite unique tie. On a pretty, dun-coloured ground is repeated several times a "liberty" horse at a stately gallop while a beautiful "equestrienne" pirouettes in the air above it. Clearly, however, the young lady must not be turned topsy-turvy, and researches go to show that therefore she must not appear on the knot but only below it. This involves some experiments a little trying before breakfast, but after all *il faut souffrir pour être beau.*—B. D.

JULY 28ᵀᴴ, 1944

A NEW TIE

Silk was very hard to come by during the war, so when a shipment of new silk ties arrived from America, it was eagerly reported on in Country Life. *The extravagant designs are matched by the extraordinary prices.*

A NEW HAT IS popularly believed to be an alternative and a tonic to a woman, and on many men who are not otherwise given to thinking much of their clothes a new tie can have the same beneficial effect. They find it wonderfully reviving to the spirits and can enjoy this modest refreshment in exchange for a single coupon. Today there comes news from America of a new line in ties which is full of promise. They are made of parachute silk and are adorned with all

"IN STRIPED TIES PLAGIARISM IS INEVITABLE"

manner of designs such as aeroplanes, palm trees, and even, as we are told, dance-band leaders and beach scenes. Designers of ties in this country, particularly of club ties, have long since realised that the limit has been reached in the permutation and combination of stripes and that in striped ties plagiarism is inevitable. So they have taken to dotting small symbolic objects, such as roses, crowns and even elephants, upon a background of a single colour. They have never yet, however, attempted anything so elaborate as a beach scene, and the first consignment from America will be eagerly expected. Unfortunately, it must be added that these ties are selling at prices ranging from 15 to 250 dollars. The honour of wearing a dance-band leader would be very great, but most of us would find such prices prohibitive. We must reluctantly put our coupons away and keep them for mere dull socks.

MAY 31ST, 1930

THE HISTORY OF THE TOP-HAT: WITH SOME OBSERVATIONS ON ITS DEVOTEES

Stove pipes, or toppers, are now rarely seen except at weddings and races, though they were at one time used for many sports, despite their impracticality.

THE SIGHT OF a platoon of the Eton O.T.C. marching out of Common Lane with a rhythmic swinging of "tails," with the glint of glossy "toppers," and with rifles sloped across (presumably) immaculate black serge, brings home to one, in one violently arresting contrast, the great problem of the top-hat, with all the questions of aesthetics and utility of athletics and ceremonial which it involves. Few fashions in masculine headgear have been as much satirised and denounced, and at the same time so long adhered to, as the top-hat. Described as "the ugliest European headdress known" and rarely mentioned in print without opprobrious epithets, such as "absurd" and "unhealthy," one would have supposed the "topper" doomed to early extinction.

> "ONE WOULD HAVE SUPPOSED THE 'TOPPER' DOOMED TO EARLY EXTINCTION"

But, on the contrary, it has – literally – flourished for over a hundred years without intermission, and the rising generation, typified by Eton and Westminster, shows no desire to cast it off. Such powers of endurance in the face of unsparing caricature and volumes of condemnation provoke the reflection that, like "the soul of goodness in things evil," there must be some inherent excellence in the top-hat which has commended it to successive generations of wearers.

MAY 10TH, 1946

THE BEARDED TIDE

WHEN, IF EVER, will the cry of "Beaver" be heard from ill-mannered lips as a bearded gentleman goes by? There is seldom the opportunity nowadays, though during the wartime the young and bearded naval officer was sometimes to be seen. It may be, however, that the whirligig of time will soon bring beards in again since Professor Murdoch of the University of Western Australia believes he has detected a psychological tide in this matter which ebbs and flows. The Elizabethans, he points outs, wore beards, since their intellects were so alert that they had no time to shave. So with the Victorians "life was real, life was earnest," and again the crucial few minutes every morning could not be spared. On the other hand, between those two periods came the more leisurely one of the eighteenth century, and what the late Mr. Frank Richardson used to describe as "face fungus" was ruthlessly destroyed. The theory is an interesting one, but the duller explanation is at least possible that the temptation to avoid shaving is much less than it used to be, since to-day's implements are so much better adapted to their purpose. We might have had a Shakespeare shaven and shorn if safety razors had been on sale at Stratford-on-Avon.

> "WITH THE VICTORIANS 'LIFE WAS REAL, LIFE WAS EARNEST,' AND THE CRUCIAL FEW MINUTES EVERY MORNING COULD NOT BE SPARED..."

AUGUST 5ᵀᴴ, 1949

REPRESSED BRACES

The morality of wearing braces is discussed in detail.

THE WARM WEATHER has posed for most men a nice – or perhaps a not nice – problem, that at first sight is not readily definable as between ethics, aesthetics, morals, structure, or calorifics. It is whether braces (suspenders to American readers) are presentable. In Britain the view appears to be that they are less so than belts, though here the issue is complicated by conflicting evidence on the relative coolness and efficiency of suspension and peripheral support, which, of course, introduces the element of mathematics – the circumference of a circle and all that. But,

> "NO ONE CAN DENY BRACES' FITNESS FOR PURPOSE"

assuming their co-efficiency, why is it that in many walks of life – on golf courses, for instance – belt-expression is tolerable while braces must be suppressed, concealed, glossed over? No one can deny braces' fitness for purpose. Regarded as a structural member, the modern brace is, in many cases, a fine thing, designed to sustain tension to the safety limit with a minimum of material. It may be this very quality of streamlining which makes braces distasteful, like some modern architecture, to the traditional mind. Yet would the Central European or Alpine species, to which all the resources of craftsmanship have been applied, enriching them into veritable works of art, be any more acceptable? It is good to know that researches into the problem are being conducted by a working party of the National Association of Brace, Belt and Suspender Manufacturers. We hazard the notion that brace-repression will be found to be a fundamental vestigial inhibition in Western civilisation, due to the principle of suspension's never having been outwardly expressed in the whole historical evolution of costume.

NOVEMBER 19ᵀᴴ, 1910

THE MODERN MAN'S DRESS

SOME DAYS AGO a correspondent wrote to a contemporary bewailing the vast change that had come over the dress of the modern man. He had been to the Park, to dinner parties, to the theatres, and other haunts of the man of fashion, and found that a great change had taken place. We ought to explain that he had been absent from England and returned to it after a period of years.

He seems to think that whatever eccentricities might be indulged in when a man was in the company of his own sex only would be laid aside when he joined the ladies. It is almost pathetic to read his description of the modern man in evening clothes. "Turn-down collars, with black ties and even coloured waistcoats were to be seen." This "even coloured waistcoats" is written in the very eloquence of horror, but it only prepares for something worse to follow. "I noticed," goes on the writer, "one individual wearing black boots with brown uppers." Here he seems to have become speechless, although he subsequently revived sufficiently

to lay down the law with a kind of magisterial scorn. "One would have thought it quite unnecessary," he says, "to point out that evening dress consists of a swallow-tailed coat, white or black waistcoat, trousers of the same material as the coat, a white tie, white kid gloves and patent-leather Oxford shoes." It reads as if he believed there was a law of the Medes and Persians ordaining that masculine members of the human race, as long as rivers fall and wind blows, to use an old expression, should in the evening don a swallow-tailed coat. He evidently thinks that to go into polite society without this garment is sufficient to cause a contusion of Nature; yet, all unconsciously, he supplies the key to his own riddle when he admits that the evening jacket is comfortable. Comfort cannot exist side-by-side with worry and the end and ideal of the dress of today is that it should be comfortable. If the critic compared the elaborate bowings and ceremonials of even thirty years ago with the easy salute, or want of salute, that is considered sufficient today, he would find more food for reflection and more changes that had been accomplished in identically the same spirit.

"MASCULINE MEMBERS OF THE HUMAN RACE SHOULD IN THE EVENING DON A SWALLOW-TAILED COAT"

NOVEMBER 28TH, 1925

CAMOUFLAGE

To the Editor of "Country Life."

Sir, —I enclose a photograph of a local sportsman who recently died at Preston. He frequently used this curious suit when out shooting, and told me that it often brought him great success. He used it in conjunction with a home-made rattle when calling up corncrakes. He was the author of an interesting book called "The Bullet Crossbow," which you may have come across.—Stanley Crook

> "HE USED IT IN CONJUNCTION WITH A HOME-MADE RATTLE WHEN CALLING UP CORNCRAKES"

[Suits of this nature are quite frequently used by professional wildfowlers on the East Coast, and are most useful when one is stalking curlew or lying up in a gun pit. We are afraid, however, that such a suit, even when used with a rattle, would be of little use to-day for calling up the corncrake, for this bird seems to be decreasing with lamentable rapidity.—Ed]

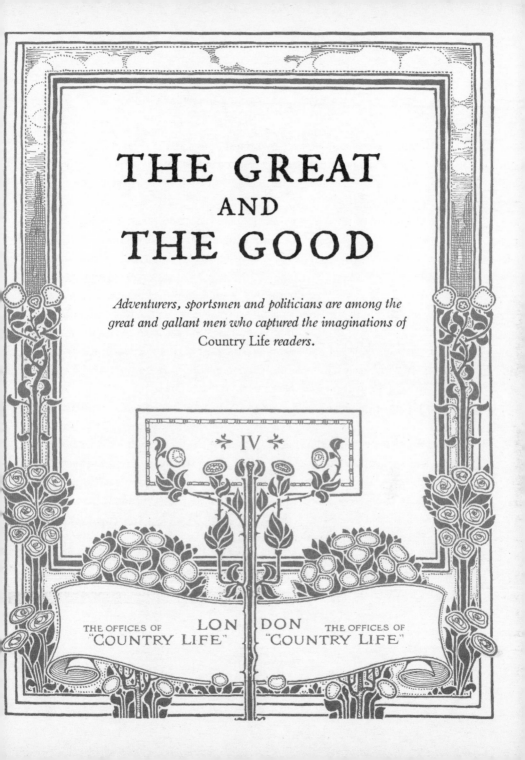

THE GREAT
AND
THE GOOD

*Adventurers, sportsmen and politicians are among the
great and gallant men who captured the imaginations of
Country Life readers.*

✣ IV ✣

THE OFFICES OF   LON DON   THE OFFICES OF
"COUNTRY LIFE"   "COUNTRY LIFE"

JULY 23RD, 1919

W. G. GRACE

'The Champion' who broke every record and, alongside Sir Donald Bradman, remains the most famous and important cricketer ever to have lived. It is difficult to exaggerate his influence on Victorian society.

FOR THOSE WHO knew "W. G.", or saw him play, the happiest spirit in which to read his biography is one of frank hero-worship. There are many things which we knew before and yet must impress us afresh. There is, for instance, the passionate devotion of the whole Grace family to the game, the picture of the practice ground in the orchard with the three dogs played in aid of the fielding, the small boy acquiring in earliest boyhood the groundwork of a vigilant defence, the old mother who never wearied in teaching and hated a left-hand batsman.

"HE OUGHT TO BE MADE TO PLAY WITH A LITTLER BAT"

Many of us may have forgotten at what an early age "W. G." became a power in the land. When he was fifteen he made 170 against the Gentlemen of Sussex. A year later – and how odd it seems to read of that Colossus as a "lean" and "lanky" boy – he was playing for the Gentlemen against the Players. Two years later again Tom Emmett was asked what he thought of him. "It's all very well against this South Country bowling," said Yorkshireman. "Let him come to Sheffield against me and George."

"W. G" went to Sheffield and made 122, and Emmett was asked his opinion again. He answered, "I call him a non-such: he ought to be made to play with a littler bat." Praise can scarcely go higher.

JUNE 2ND, 1900

MAJOR-GENERAL BADEN-POWELL – THE MANY-SIDED

ENERAL BADEN-POWELL, "The Man of the Hour," the gallant commander and defender of Mafeking, is an excellent example of the saying that it is "the busy man who finds time for everything." He never wastes a minute of his time, and seems to be able to do with less sleep than other people even, for in India he managed to do more than anyone on five hours' sleep in the night and none at all during the daytime in the hottest of summers.

JANUARY 18ᵀᴴ, 1941

B.-P. AT HOME: RECOLLECTIONS OF THE CHIEF SCOUT AS NEIGHBOUR AND COUNTRYMAN

BY MAJOR A. G. WADE

"GOD MADE THE COUNTRYSIDE, the devil made the towns."
The late Lord Baden-Powell accepted the truth of the saying, and never was the devil attacked in a more vital spot than when B.-P. took Scouting into the slums of our great cities.

> "HE HAD A NIGHTMARE LEST SOME CHILD IN BENTLEY SHOULD BE FORGOTTEN AND GO TO BED ON CHRISTMAS NIGHT WITHOUT HAVING HAD A TOY"

B.-P. had time for everything. The River Wey that forms the parish boundary in the south needed cleaning out, and re-stocking with trout. In days gone by these Hampshire chalk streams used to abound with trout: B.-P. set himself at once to restock the water. Passers-by, too, must often have noticed the Bentley village sign which he was largely responsible for designing and erecting.

Even the humblest cottager was known by him, and if he saw a little cottage garden emerging out of what had been a dirty ash-strewn plot he used to write a note saying he was glad to see another garden in Bentley and that, in case the judges at the annual prize-giving for the best-kept gardens had overlooked this one, would the owner please accept the enclosed 10.s. as an extra prize?

Christmas was an anxious time for B.-P. He had a nightmare lest some child in Bentley should be forgotten and go to bed on Christmas night without having had a toy. And so, after tea on Christmas Day he used to come to me and we would go round the cottages where there were children. With him he brought large sacks of surplus toys and outside the cottage doors we used to leave a bundle, knocking on the door before we left. He never showed himself on these occasions; the knock was to make sure that the presents would be taken in.

His property, Pax Hill, was open house, all day, to all the world, and all the world came to see "the world's greatest schoolmaster." *The Times's* leading article, recording the death and doings of B.-P., ends with the words, "he has had far too little recognition for all that he has done." This was not entirely the world's fault, for he shunned publicity, unless it was for the work that he had in hand, and occasionally there was a puckish manner in his self-effacement. I remember an occasion when, dressed as he generally was in very elderly clothes, some strangers coming up the drive mistook him for the gardener and enquired if Lord Baden-Powell was at Home. Sizing up those particular visitors, B.-P. replied that he was afraid he was out.

THE LAST DESPATCH FROM EVEREST

The mystery of whether Mallory and Irvine reached the top of Everest is still pondered today. Here is the contemporary report.

IN THE RECORDS of mountaineering, Mr. Odell's story of the final attempt on Mount Everest will always hold a most important place. The writer was the only member of the expedition who actually saw Mallory and Irvine attempting the last climb.

On 6th June Mallory and Irvine, "after joyfully having a breakfast of fried sardines," of which they partook in moderation, started for Camp V (25,000 ft.) accompanied by porters carrying provisions and reserve oxygen cylinders. Using oxygen they had already ascended to Camp III, a distance of 2,000 ft. in a couple of hours, which they considered good going.

"IF YOUTH, ENERGY, PLUCK AND DETERMINATION COULD MAKE A HERO THEN HE WAS ONE"

That night porters brought back a message from Mallory. It seems to have been a confident little note, showing that all had gone well so far. Up to 27,000 ft. they had used only the minimum oxygen, and the weather was perfect. Something of the pleasure it gave Odell is reflected in his word picture of the outlook from his lofty camp and of a great sunset; westward a savage jumble of peaks culminating in Cho Uyo (26,750 ft.) and right opposite "the giant cliffs of Everest."

One glimpse of the climbers was given him on the morning of June 8th. He beheld them as only two black dots on the snowy landscape. There is nothing impossible or improbable in the narrator's surmise that the two climbers may have realised their ambition to reach the top of the mountain.

Nothing was omitted in the way of search to determine what had happened. It will ever be a mystery whether they succeeded or not in reaching the summit, but were the mystery to be penetrated, it would make little difference to the fame of these young mountaineers. If youth, energy, pluck and determination could make a hero then he was one.

MALLORY AS HE WILL BE REMEMBERED

MALLORY WAS a singularly handsome young fellow with a really wonderful face, which, together with his well-knit athletic figure, gave him an outward charm which was only equalled by the charm of his mind and of his spirit. He was always very popular with all who knew him and he had a very wide circle of acquaintances. Recently he had become heir to an estate at Moberley in the north of England, and he had, in many ways, the world at his feet.

But only those who were really intimate with him knew another, and a more spiritual, side of his character. He was very introspective, and lived apart in a world of ideals, and those ideals were of the highest. He was deeply serious in his outlook, and he took little interest in trivial matters, so that if the conversation, which forms so large a part of an undergraduate's education, wandered away, as it must do in time, from the high plane he used to set, he invariably tried to draw it back to the level from which it had fallen. He was essentially honest in thought and in deed and at times outspoken – so outspoken, in fact, that a momentary irritation was sometimes produced; but that invariably passed away and was immediately forgotten.

One could not help feeling when one heard of his death among the snows and storms of the unconquered mountain that –

> Heav'n lifts her everlasting portals high
> And bids the pure in heart behold their God.

—A. E. SHIPLEY

[In a note to Sir Arthur Shipley's brief but perfect appreciation it is sufficient to recall the circumstances of Mallory's death as far as they are,

or are ever likely to be, known. He and his companion Irvine when last seen were toiling up the last 1,000 ft. of Everest and "going strong." What arrested their progress when so close to the summit of their desire, no one knows, as neither signal nor token was received from them afterwards. They may have dropped exhausted in the snow, or have been victims of one of those unexpected accidents which attend high mountaineering. We know that they could not have survived for two nights without shelter at that altitude and amid such desolation.—Ed]

APRIL 14TH, 1928

LORD HAILSHAM

Douglas Hogg served as Lord Chancellor during two Conservative governments, from 1928 to 1929 and 1935 to 1938, and was renowned for his cross-examination and debating skills.

H E HAS PLAYED football for Eton; he has beaten the champion fencer of the day, he has served as a clerk in the City, and as a trooper in South Africa; and, though he was only called to the Bar at thirty, he will be remembered as the best all-round advocate of his time. Whether he was arguing an arid point of law at the later of their Lordships' House, or cross-examining for fraud in the special jury court, or prosecuting spies and Communists, at the Old Bailey, or even moving a quiet motion in a gentlemanly equity style in the Chancery Division, he was a master of his art and a match for any opponent. At the Bar, where there are so many specialists, he did not specialise; in life, on the other hand, he is *par excellence* a specialist. He might be said to have fewer interests in life than most men of distinction, but those he has are stronger and more powerful than in any man I know.

A stranger meeting him socially would, probably, think he was addressing a very ingenuous and exceedingly modest man, who never pushed his view forward unless it was asked for. He would credit him with little knowledge of life. He has even been described as "a slightly bucolic figure." But woe to that man if he found himself in the witness box under cross-examination by Douglas Hogg! Although the Lord Chancellor's rule in cross-examination was never to ask a question unless he knew the answer, the witness would find that there was little about his character and motives which Douglas Hogg did not know and was not able to use against him. Perhaps his greatest triumph in this line was when he made the plaintiff in a libel action apologise in open court for the dreadful things he had said about the defendant! He has been described as a man of the strictest principle, whose principles enter into his daily life. He has a host of enthusiastic admirers but few close friends and, even in the Socialist Party, no enemies.—A. P.

SEPTEMBER 29TH, 1923

THE LATE MARQUESS OF RIPON

THAT THE MARQUESS of Ripon was the finest shot of his generation has been stated so often and backed by such abundant proof that it has become one of the accepted canons of game shooting. To do a thing well is to gain high gratification, but to do it better than anyone else in the world is to assume a heavy burden as well as to probe satisfaction to its greatest depths.

Out of hundreds there could never be more than a few dozens in possession of the gifts and attainments needful to place them in the highest rank of all. To enumerate those at the very top of the shooting tree would necessitate the discussion of about fifty names, yet never was there any question as to who occupied the topmost branch. It was

> "THE FINEST SHOT OF HIS GENERATION"

always Earl de Grey, whose physique could stand the buffet of countless rounds, who would undergo rigorous drill on the lawn beforehand with his two loaders and three guns, whose lightning speed of alignment was never hustled to the extent of that fraction of a second which spoils the result, whose eye could pick out the birds in the best order for shooting, and whose skill continued relentlessly throughout the flush. These and other circumstances made him the one man who possessed all the equipment, inherent and acquired, needed for shooting.

Just as the conditions which provided his opportunity grew into being during his own adolescence, so they reached their climax during his middle life of greatest vigour; and alas! their decadence – we hope only temporary – synchronised with the passing of his own meridian.

NOVEMBER 22ND, 1924

JACK LONDON

EIGHT YEARS AGO today, on November 22nd, 1916, Jack London died. When all the heavens were lurid with the light of battle fires, the passing of this bright star, that had twinkled for the English-speaking nations for seventeen years went, comparatively speaking, unnoticed: but the loss to the world was greater, possibly, than this generation can measure. The many facets he had displayed already had not, apparently, exhausted the resources of his brain, for when he died, in his forty-first year, he, the expounder of man's physical nature, was turning more and more to the psychological aspects of humanity. He had at least thirty years more of work before him, had he continued the vigorous physical pursuits which rejoiced his youth and made his manhood virile; but, although he had read and applauded John Masefield's "Everlasting Mercy," he had forgotten the couplet:

> "THE UNKNOWN CALLED TO HIM EVER, THE UNKNOWN OF SEA AND LAND, OF MIND AND MATTER..."

For life be joy, and mind is fruit,
And body's precious earth sad root.

Descended from English stock, the great-great-grandson of an English baronet, Sir William London, it is no wonder that Jack London was compounded of the exploring stuff which has gone to the making of the British Empire. The Unknown called to him ever, the unknown of sea and land, of mind and matter, and there were few phases of human activity which in his abbreviated life he did not explore. When little more than a schoolboy he was "King of the Oyster Pirates" in San Francisco Bay. At seventeen he was drawing man's pay on a sealer, the *Sophie Sutherland*, in which he sailed around half the world. When the insistent urge of curiosity turned him inland, he became a "hobo," a tramp, jumping freight trains, "telling the tale," fraternising with the down-and-outs, draining to the last dregs – even to imprisonment for vagrancy – the cup of knowledge which the grimy hand of the human pariahs held out to him. Ever a boy – even in his last year of life.

DECEMBER 12TH, 1925

RUDYARD KIPLING

I N THE FROSTY fall of the year Rudyard Kipling has become gravely
ill, and all England, young and old, has been anxious for him. We are
happy in the hope that the worst has now passed – that our great
national writer will be spared to us for many years.

Our uncrowned kings of letters have generally been greater than our
crowned. Kipling never was laureate, but he wears the invisible laurel.
He has been our most representative literary man during the twentieth
century. Carlyle, Tennyson, Kipling
seem in true sequence, voices of England
heard not by ourselves alone, but by the
people of the empire and the world.

"OUR UNCROWNED KINGS OF LETTERS"

If one were directing a foreigner as to which author to study to
gain knowledge of England it would not be good advice to send him to
Dickens, so excellent in his day, nor to Mr. Chesterton and Mr. Shaw. It
is Rudyard Kipling that we should place in his hands.

In his way Kipling has remained as democratic and as much a man of
the people as any Labour man. For instance, he and the late Will Crooks
would have got on very well together. But strong-worded as is Kipling's
contribution to our literature, strident as is his voice, one should realise a
very humble, noble soul behind it all, one utterly worthy of the national
affection which goes out to him at this time.

> The tumult and the shouting dies
> The captains and the Kings depart,
> Still stands Thine ancient sacrifice
> An humble and a contrite heart.

—STEPHEN GRAHAM

THE DEATH OF ERNEST SHACKLETON

Ernest Shackleton was, together with Scott, one of Britain's most celebrated Antarctic adventurers.

THE WHOLE COUNTRY was deeply moved on Monday by the announcement of Sir Ernest Shackleton's death. It was dramatic in its unexpectedness. Sir Ernest was almost at the beginning of his great task, the *Quest* had only got as far as the coast of South Georgia. His health had given no cause for anxiety since his departure from England. In a letter received by his friend Mr. John Quiller Rowett, who was mainly responsible for financing the *Quest* expedition, written from Rio on December 5th, he said: "The next you will hear will be, please God, success," and that should anything untoward happen it would not be due to the ship, which seems to have satisfied him in every way. His high courage may be guessed from the two lines with which he closes his letter: "Never for me the lowered burner. Never the lost endeavour."

"AN EPIC OF BRITISH PLUCK AND RESOLUTION AND ENDURANCE"

But at half-past three in the morning of January 5th he called Major Macklin and complained of a pain in the back. Major Macklin called Dr. McIllroy, but Sir Ernest died within three minutes, before anything could be done. He had recently recovered from an attack of influenza, and had complained of feeling tired and unwell when he went to bed. It is as sad as sad can be. Sir Ernest had drawn up a great programme for exploring a part of the Antarctic region hitherto unknown. We all know the energy and organising power with which he got the expedition ready. No one knew better than he the risks of the journey he had undertaken, for there was no man in Great Britain who had sterner experience of travel near the Southern Pole. Before this expedition he had been on three others. Indeed, from youth onward he had manifested those qualities which make a great explorer. He faced danger and difficulty for their own sakes and was resolved almost from infancy not to subside into merely respectable home-staying citizen.

When a full life of Shackleton comes to be written, it will be an epic of British pluck and resolution and endurance. He possessed to the full the dogged character of the seaman who laid the foundation of England's greatness.

MAY 11ᵀᴴ, 1918

CAPTAIN BALL, HERO OF THE AIR

EW WILL READ the story of Captain Ball's short career ("Captain Ball, V.C." by Walter A. Briscoe and H. Russell Stannard; Jenkins) without feeling its pathos as we are admiring its brilliance. From beginning to end he was such a boy. His love of merriment never flagged nor his gaiety ceased. He fought his air-battles as an English youth plays cricket, resolute, very keen for his side, but bearing no trace of ill-will to opponents even when most determined to beat them.

> **"HE FOUGHT HIS AIR-BATTLES AS AN ENGLISH YOUTH PLAYS CRICKET..."**

Nothing is more typical of him than the account of his battle with a Hun as keen as himself. Each tried every device he knew against the other, and the battle went on till the ammunition of both was exhausted. "There was nothing more to be done after that," said Ball, "so we both burst out laughing. We flew side by side, laughing at each other for a few seconds, and then we waved adieu to each other and went oft."

In a letter to his father he said: "I only scrap because it is my duty, but I do not think anything bad about the Hun. He is just a good chap with very little guts, trying to do his best." But this was only frankness in a family letter. To his brother officers he was, as one of them expressed it, "a tiger to fight, a Hotspur of the twentieth century." A single letter is all we have room for, but what a picture it gives of the boy's high spirit, his splendid fighting, and his unquenchable energy:

"My Dearest Mother and Dad.

"Cheerio, dears. And, oh, the wind blows good out here. Do so hope it is the same with you.

"Really, I am having too much luck for a boy. I will start straight away, and tell you all. On August 22nd I went up. Met twelve Huns.

"No. 1 fight. I attacked and fired two drums, bringing the machine down just outside a village. All crashed up.

"No. 2 fight. I attacked and got under machine, putting in two drums. Hun went down in flames.

"No. 3 fight. I attacked and put in one drum. Machine went down and crashed on a housetop.

"I only got hit eleven times in the planes, so I returned and got more ammunition. This time luck was not all on the spot. I was met by about 14 Huns, about 15 miles over their side. My wind screen was hit in four places, mirror broken, the spar of the left plane broken, also engine ran out of petrol. But I had good sport and good luck, but only just for I was brought down about one mile over our side. I slept near the machine and had it repaired during the night."

Captain Ball died on 7th May, 1917

MARCH 1ST, 1913

DR. E. A. WILSON

"Uncle Bill", as Dr. Wilson was affectionately known, accompanied Scott on his last and fatal expedition as chief of scientific staff.

THE PATHETIC STORY of Captain Scott's Expedition has profoundly moved the whole world. But the gloom which it has occasioned is relieved by the account of the splendid fortitude which this band of heroes displayed as they saw their dreadful end approaching. Not yet have we come into possession of all the facts concerning the tragedy, but when we do, we suspect we shall hear more of Dr. E. A. Wilson, who died at his leader's side. Dr. Wilson was one of the most lovable of men. He was also a most enthusiastic and accomplished zoologist, and no mean artist, he made splendid additions to our knowledge of the seals and whales of the Antarctic, and his accounts of the life-histories of the Adelié and Emperor penguins were even more valuable because circumstances enabled him to make them more complete.

North Polar Bear.

It has been asked more than once during the last few days "Is the information to be obtained by such perilous expeditions worth the sacrifice it entails?" The answer is emphatically, Yes. Captain Scott and the gallant band who accompanied him most certainly thought so. We are apt today to value all enterprises by their possible commercial returns. But that is an unworthy standard. Knowledge is power, and a deeper knowledge of the mysteries of Nature is beyond all price. Moreover, the so-called "useless" knowledge of one generation proves to be of the most vital importance to the next.

"IS THE INFORMATION TO BE OBTAINED BY SUCH PERILOUS EXPEDITIONS WORTH THE SACRIFICE IT ENTAILS?"

Those who knew him well have suffered a loss which is irreparable. Science has lost a devoted disciple, but the world at large has gained an example of how to live and how to die that

is worth striving to imitate. He fell in a battle with the elements in striving to extend the boundaries of knowledge. What more glorious end could a man desire?

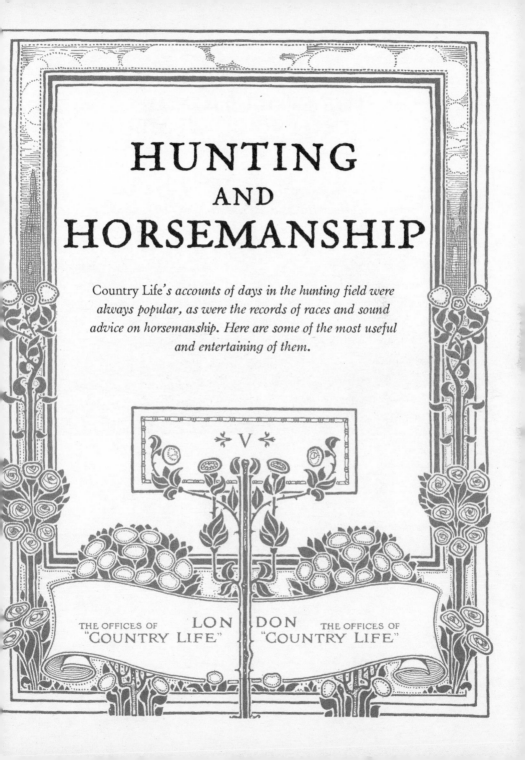

HUNTING
AND
HORSEMANSHIP

Country Life's accounts of days in the hunting field were
always popular, as were the records of races and sound
advice on horsemanship. Here are some of the most useful
and entertaining of them.

❖ V ❖

THE OFFICES OF   LON DON   THE OFFICES OF
"COUNTRY LIFE"   "COUNTRY LIFE"

DECEMBER 8TH, 1923

THE EVOLUTION OF HUNTING COSTUME

BY LIONEL EDWARDS

*Lionel Edwards, most famous for his paintings of hunting scenes,
was a regular contributor to* Country Life's *columns on hunting and
horsemanship. Here are his thoughts on what to wear in the field.*

IT IS RATHER a remarkable fact that there seems to be a singular lack of anything dealing with the sporting costume of our ancestors. It is surprising how frequently hunting costume has changed in detail, if not, perhaps, in essentials, during its comparatively modern career. For, compared with stag and hare hunting, fox hunting is essentially a modern sport.

It is still a debated point who first entered a pack of hounds to fox hunting. Some say Lord Arundel in 1690, others Mr. Thomas Boothby of Tooley Park, Leicestershire.

Huntsmen's costume had changed by 1810. Judging by the prints of T. Oldaker (after Ben Marshall) and others, he was by this time wearing his own hair (unpowdered). The coat has become even more like a dressing-gown, covering his knee and much of his boot, and the stirrup leather has shifted from round his waist to round his shoulder, as at present worn by whips and second horsemen.

By 1820 there is a curious change. The hunting cap is quite different, the peak going round to the side and even back in less proportion. It is, in fact, more helmet-shaped, with a ribbon round it tied at the back.

By 1828–30 a very modern-looking hunting cap has appeared, and the huntsman's coat has shortened to above the knee. In one of Will Long on Bertha, in the possession of the Duke of Beaufort, the coat, except for the high and rolled collar, might be that of a modern hunt servant. The breeches appear to have been skin-tight at this period, and the foot-gear more top than boot!

As an example of eccentricity, take Jack Lambert, huntsman to the Cottesmore, who always wore a top hat, and Shaw, huntsman to the Duke of Rutland, who never came to the meet with his hounds, but hacked on in style. In a print of Aiken's his valet is seen removing his gaiters, which he wore to protect his immaculate breeches and tops.

Whips varied tremendously. They were often "carried upside down," according to our ideas! They were frequently of iron or brass and hammer-headed. I have several such, and very unwieldy and badly balanced they are. Their purpose was the breaking of padlocks on locked gates, and for protection from footpads and highwaymen – so, at least, it is said. The Heythrop Hunt servants carried whips of this type until quite recently. Possibly, they still do so.

IMPRESSIONS OF THE PRINCE OF WALES' FIRST STEEPLECHASE

T HE PARTICIPATION IN a Point-to-Point race by the Prince of Wales is a pleasant and interesting event and must not be allowed to pass without some reference. It has, indeed, raised the public admiration for one who has already a deep hold on popular affection. People see in the Heir Apparent a young Englishman full to overflowing of the highest traditions in sport, an ardent lover of horses and the chase, and one who is irresistibly attracted to anything in which there is an element of risk, even of danger.

I do not think he liked his job, to begin with, and if the Prince had to ride the race over again, he would probably get hold of the horse rather more vigorously at the start and slip him into the first fence or two. What happened was that he had so much confidence in the horse as to leave it to him. Thus the horse screwed a bit at the first fence and probably because he did not altogether like it he slipped into the second one so unshipping the Prince.

"HE SLIPPED INTO THE SECOND ONE SO UNSHIPPING THE PRINCE..."

After a brief chase horse and rider came together again, but by this time Lord Dalmeny and four or five others, including Lieutenant-Colonel Lord Henry Seymour, were two fields or more ahead. It was then that the Prince really asserted himself. He used his whip to such effect as to send Pet Dog about his business at the next fence – by no means a pretty one looked at from the ground – and, thereafter, all was fairly plain sailing to a horseman unafraid of the jumps ahead and of using his horse's speed to the utmost across the pasture, ridge and furrow.

He began to close the gap in great style, and with another half mile or so to go he would probably have won. As it was he had to accept third place behind Captain the Earl of Dalkeith and Lord Henry Seymour.

Lord Dalmeny fell when leading not far from home. I think it was his horse that let the Prince down (in more senses than one) in the early stages. He evidently wanted *fortiter in re* methods at the outset, and if they had been used he would have been straightened out at the early fences and made to jump properly; but as to the Prince's horsemanship and valour I have nothing but the highest praise.

MARCH 24TH, 1923

AT THE GRAND MILITARY

To the Editor of "Country Life."

Sir,—I hope you may like to see these original silhouettes, which represent a few of my impressions of the Grand Military Meeting at Sandown Park last Saturday. I should be very glad if you thought that they will prove of any interest to the readers of Country Life.—Ethel Murle

FEBRUARY 9ᵀᴴ, 1924

THE APPROACH

BY LIEUT.-COLONEL M. F. McTAGGART, D.S.O.

A poetic approach is taken to jumping fences.

WHAT IS THE secret of presenting a horse at a fence so that he will jump it off his hocks, land a comfortable distance the other side, and give us what is known as a "good feel"? The first necessity is to have a temperate horse. Our first essential is control. Our second is that of growing momentum, so that when we have decided to "put" our horse at the fence (which is at a distance of about 10 ft., or so, according to the size of the jump), each stride from there should be of increasing dimension. In this way we get the impetus on taking off to throw us well into the next field, clear of all hidden ditches and other abominations. It can well be described as:

Umpty, umpty, umpty, one, two, three, over!

In other words a steady canter up to the last three strides, and then one – two – THREE. Diagrammatically we can show it thus:

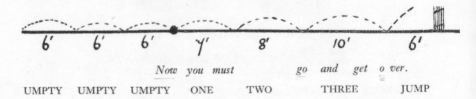

| 6′ | 6′ | 6′ | 7′ | 8′ | 10′ | 6′ |

Now you must *go and get o ver.*

| UMPTY | UMPTY | UMPTY | ONE | TWO | THREE | JUMP |

This is, of course, perfection. We have control up to the obstacle, and a pleasurable land 12 ft. the other side. That is what we should endeavour to do with every fence we meet out hunting. We shall not succeed, but with practice and training we shall improve every day. We shall not always be able to make three good strides. We may have to fit it in with two. It rather reminds me of dactyls and spondees. We may have a long and two shorts, two shorts and a long, perhaps, or two longs. We might even make up Latin verses as we go along. To hear the huntsman chant:

‾ " " ‾ " "
"Arma vir/umque can/o"

or a whipper in mutter:

" " ‾ " " ‾ " " "
"Vide/o meli/ora pro/boque"

on approaching their fence would be an inspiring novelty! And yet we require our cadences just as much in equitation as in elegiacs. Fortunately for many of us, an equally good result can be obtained in English, and I can suggest the following exhortation, with mental rather than vocal expression, and an increasing accent on the "longs," thus:

‾ " " ‾ " " ‾ "
"Now you must / go and get / over."

This gives a good idea of the final strides with the spring on the first syllable of "over". But we shall not find it always possible to try it in the hunting field. We shall often find that the crowd will not give us room, and we have to get over as best we may. Sometimes we will find that when we want to go "umpty" the horse does not. Sometime he will "yaw" at us and drag the reins through our fingers. Sometimes he will insist on racing at the fence and we shall be unable to restrain him. But no matter, as long as we know what we want to do.

OCTOBER 6ᵀᴴ, 1928

BRIGHTER ELEVENSES

The pitfalls of hosting the Meet are discussed – should a large breakfast be served, or can guests make do with cherry brandy and salted cod?

EVERYONE WHO COMES to a Meet meaning (hunting) business will be to some extent preoccupied, and the result will inevitably be a certain forcing of cheerfulness. Host and hostess are dismally aware that they are never really at their best at eleven o' clock in the morning, and that, anyhow, you can't be in two places at once. If you stay in the house, you fail to give a welcome to those idiots outside, who refuse to come in, even for a moment. If you go outside to join the other idiots, you are not in the house when you are wanted.

It is bad enough for the host and hostess, but for the non-hunting spectator it is a situation quite appalling for its missing of opportunity. One cannot but sympathise with an outsider's disappointment, and one cannot but agree that, in these days, when the solid Hunt breakfast is, mercifully, a thing of the past, the hasty snatching of a cigarette and cherry brandy makes but a scrubby opening to this great and hazardous emprise – the history of which is bound up in that of England itself.

Do let us try not to be muddle-headed about it. After all, this hunting entertainment would be either a wicked extravagance or the grossest sentimentality unless it had some solid ideal behind it. What, then, is the *object* of our kind host and hostess? Surely when you really get down to it their whole aim and ambition is to turn their foodstuffs and drinkstuffs into energy – and so to have, vicariously, their humble (but admirable) share in some at least of those Catherine wheels which bold and energetic horsemen will shortly be turning. Very well. I am no great housekeeper, and I am not going to lay down for hostesses exactly what items should be eliminated from their present generous, but over-lavish list of things they give us to eat and drink. I will only say this – the fuel value of fresh cod is 220 calories per lb., against 325 for the salted (the carbohydrates in both being nil). It is only a suggestion; but when, with all three bands playing, you next walk into the house to get your cherry brandy – and when you *do* get your plate of nice salted cod or something of the kind – why, then, you will, perhaps, think kindly of me as you come quickly out again to get on your horse bristling with energy and other things.— CRASCREDO

OCTOBER 18ᵀᴴ, 1902

BROOK JUMPING

OST MEN, on their return from hunting, will tell us where the hounds ran to, the length of the chase, and whether it was fast or slow. But on the fences they say nothing. Either they have jumped them much as the obstacles came, or they have shirked. In the first case the hedges and ditches are a matter of course; in the second we none of us talk more than we can help about what we have not done. But if there is a brook in the line, more particularly if it be historic like the Rosy in Berkshire, the Chearsley in the Bicester and the Whissendine, Stonton, Smite, or Swift in Leicestershire, and if we have jumped over it successfully, we can scarcely help alluding to the feat, or hoping that someone else will do so.

"IF OUR PLUCK IS RIGHT AND WE REALLY MEAN TO TRY, THE HORSE WILL NOT FIND US OUT"

On the whole I should think that fewer serious accidents happen at brooks than at any other kind of obstacle. "True," the cynic may say, "because fewer men try to jump over them." Horses dislike water very often, and their aversion to it is reasonable, for we think horses are more often hurt or stunned in leaping, or failing to leap a brook than at any other kind of jump.

It has been said that thorough-bred horses dislike water jumping more than others, but, be this as it may, when they consent they are the best and safest at it. The speed to which they can attain without going too fast, the length of their stride, and the natural courage and boldness of a blood horse when roused, often carry them easily over large brooks.

But as we come into the field where the line of willows marks the brook, or we see the hounds disappear and then pause to shake themselves as they climb out on the further bank, we may sit down quite still, drop our hands, and let the horse go at a fair pace. This should not be forced, but if the horse is keen it may be slightly steadied as we draw near. If our pluck is right and we really mean to try, the horse will not find us out. Possibly we are riding one of those brilliant horses that only care to be in the same field with the hounds.

APRIL 25TH, 1914

HUMOURS OF THE POINT-TO-POINT

NOTHING IS TRUER than the saying that "Laughter lightens labour," and the faculty of seeing the humorous side of things tends to prolong life and to lighten the burden of it generally. Few situations lend themselves more readily to the ridiculous than the back of a horse, and few people, if they would tell the truth of the matter, but would confess to having at some time or other contributed to the gaiety of their friends through the medium of some unrehearsed incident in their equestrian experience. In the hunting field, where, I think, we may take it for granted most of the capable horsemen and horsewomen are found, most days provide for the observant something which provokes a smile, and quite commonly something exceedingly funny. The wise man tempers his laughter with sympathy, knowing that his own turn may come next.

And one sees the man whose possessions are always to him the best, trying to demonstrate that a good hunter must also be a racehorse, and that his own mind and condition are good enough to last over four miles or so of country without falling off. Another sportsman pulls up his stirrup leathers several holes shorter than he is used to, in accordance with professional practice nowadays, the result very likely being that he conduces to the gaiety of the spectators by coming off on the first opportunity.

OCTOBER 6TH, 1925

WITH THE DEVON AND SOMERSET STAGHOUNDS

Following the staghounds in a motor car can be a perilous pastime –
luckily the deer in question took a good leap.

TO THE EDITOR OF "COUNTRY LIFE."

SIR,—A remarkable incident occurred a few days ago when the Devon and Somerset Staghounds met a large field at Sandyway. The tufters had not long been put into Longwood before a stag was afoot, and passing up the combe he turned right-handed up the hill towards Sandyway Cross, where a large number of foot-followers and motor cars had assembled to await eventualities. In one bound this deer crossed the North Moulton road, jumping from the fence, he cleared a motor car with its hood up and landed in safety on the far side of the road in full view of everyone.—O'B. FF.

NOVEMBER 29ᵀᴴ, 1924

WITH THE RUFFORD HUNT

An unconventional viewing point is put to good use by one of Rufford Hunt's members.

To the Editor of "Country Life."

Sɪʀ,—I send you a photograph of George Lee, the veteran runner of the Rufford Hunt. He is viewing the fox away at Kirton Wood, and, as you see, is using the backs of two plough horses for the purpose.—
Howard Barrett

HUNTING FROM LONDON

Hunting was not exclusively for those living in the country. Thanks to the railroads, even a Londoner could keep his own horse near him and still enjoy a day in the field.

THERE ARE MANY ways of hunting I have not tried – hotels, lodgings, a hunting-box, and hunting from home when I have had one. Few men have travelled more miles to snatch a day's sport in the midst of a busy life. But I do not know any time that I look back upon with more pleasure than the season I hunted from London. Many people will not agree in this, and yet there is something particularly charming about the contrast of starting from London in the early foggy morning, and finding yourself about 11 a.m. sitting beside a covert listening to the cheer of the huntsman, and hoping to hear the note of the hound.

"THE PLEASURES OF ANTICIPATION WERE KEENLY ENJOYED"

Now, to hunt successfully from town you want a placid horse, one that will stand quietly at the station while he is boxed and unboxed, and that will not take half a day's work out of himself by fretting and trembling and kicking in the box. A horse should be well clothed for a journey. Like ourselves, they like to travel warm, and like us, too they are more apt to get a chill when tired at the end of a long day. There was a special train from town for the members of the hunt, and I soon found that I had unwittingly dropped into informal membership of a very pleasant club. Very delightful when there was no sign of frost were those journeys down. The pleasures of anticipation were keenly enjoyed; never they more vivid than when training to a meet. Naturally, the men who hunt from London are keen sportsmen. If it were not so they would not take the trouble.

But a reader may ask, why not keep your horses at a more convenient centre? To that I reply that I would rather have my horses under my own eye than away, for if you have a bad groom he neglects them, and if you have a good one the independent life demoralises him. Only one thing you must have – to end as we began – a quiet horse and a good feeder. In practice I found my horses did very well. Were I a rich man I would not take a lad with me, for the lone lounge at a public with the ostlers, too often "fallen angels of servitude," is sure to be bad for him. In my flask a little dry light port, with plenty of cigars, and I really think that some of my happiest days have been spent in hunting from London.

FEBRUARY 11TH, 1911

HUNTING WITH FOOT-HARRIERS

THE MAN OR woman who hunts on foot with February beagles must be fairly athletic and in hard condition to be able to witness most of the fun. But hunting with a pack of foot-harriers calls for even greater demands on the physique of those who follow this kind of chase. To enjoy a hare-hunt in the old-fashioned manner, where the hare is not too much bustled and has time to display all those tricks and subterfuges of which she has so large an assortment, it is far better to employ the old-fashioned harrier blood, in which nose and cry have not been too much sacrificed to pace.

In a fox-hunt, where the quarry goes to the earth if he can, you must hurry all the way; a hare, on the contrary, is always above ground, and the faster you can push her, the more quickly she is killed and the worse run she affords.

JANUARY 19TH, 1924

BALANCE

BY LIEUT.-COLONEL M. F. McTAGGART, D.S.O.

THERE ARE SO many ways of sitting on a saddle, and of riding generally, that it is difficult, even for experts, to explain why one man's seat is preferable to that of another. In every art plenty of latitude must be given to individuality, and there is no art in which this is more noticeable than in that of horsemanship. Some riders achieve good results by being what are called strong riders. They remain with the horse largely by muscular effort. Others seem to succeed equally well who have no such pretensions. Some get fair results by the "crash and bang" style, and others by more delicate treatment; but few are satisfied with the results, for most of us feel there is much room for improvement.

It is generally admitted that balance is an essential and a fundamental of riding, and it is the object of this article to look into this matter and to find out if we cannot discover some clue to solution of the problem of "seat". Even though there are many ways of sitting on a saddle, we must allow there are few that can be called balanced. If the seat be not a balanced one, then connection with the saddle can only be maintained by force, either by the legs, or by the hands, or by both. If the seat be approaching a balance, the effort can be reduced, and if the balance be a true one we only require a normal and natural pressure. So, if we wish to ride comfortably we must ride balanced. There can be only three distinct fulcra from which balance can be maintained in the saddle, namely, the seat bones, the knees, and the feet.

JULY 29TH, 1911

HORSEMANSHIP IN ROTTEN ROW

THE AUTOMOBILE IS evidently no serious rival to the hack. Indeed, I am told that in Paris, since the introduction of motor-cars, riding has become more fashionable. And the trained hack even more valuable than before, and a visit to Rotten Row in the London season shows us that as a means of exercise the horse has lost none of its popularity. One can hardly lean against the rails and watch the unending procession without gaining some knowledge of the present state of horsemanship in England. The rider is of a very common type, the man or woman who corrects by the use of the hands the faults of the seat. The only thing we can say of such horsemanship is that it illustrates in an extreme form Lord Palmerston's famous dictum, "that the outside of the horse was the best thing for the inside of a man."

"THE OUTSIDE OF THE HORSE WAS THE BEST THING FOR THE INSIDE OF A MAN"

Good of its kind is the Continental seat, the short stirrups, according to our ideas, being useful in making the horse go in collected form. To use what the school riders call the "aids" with effect it would, in fact, be impossible to ride with stirrups as long as some of us do. Note, too, the powerful bit, which necessitates a certain fineness of hands; and we see one characteristic feature of the French seat in the drawing back of, and the grip given by, the lower part of the leg.

And last, but not least, is the picture of the little boy or girl making his or her first acquaintance with the Row – a child with all its riding troubles and pleasures before it. But the little fellow sits as if to the manner born, and we who have left much of our riding behind us may be pardoned if we feel a pang of envy. And so day after day the panorama of horsemanship passes us in the Row, and we realise that, after all the horse has still a future since he is still the source of pleasure and training to the generation coming on, as he has been to those in the past.

A CONTINENTAL SEAT

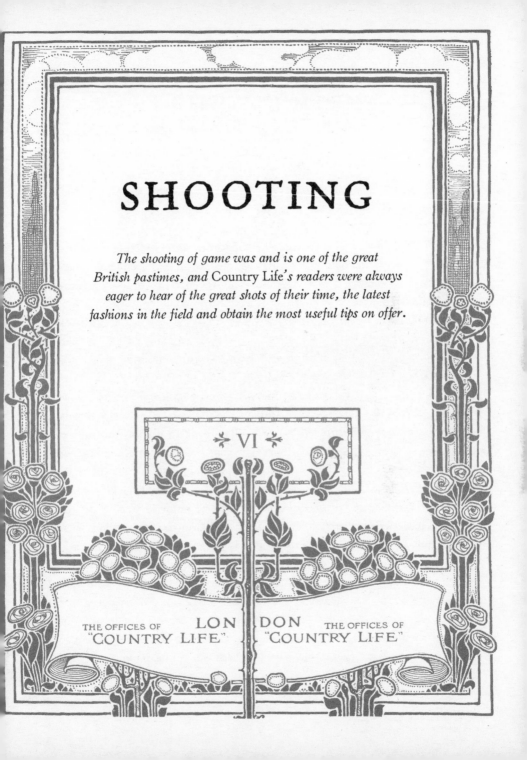

SHOOTING

The shooting of game was and is one of the great British pastimes, and Country Life's readers were always eager to hear of the great shots of their time, the latest fashions in the field and obtain the most useful tips on offer.

❖ VI ❖

THE OFFICES OF   LONDON   THE OFFICES OF
"COUNTRY LIFE"   "COUNTRY LIFE"

OCTOBER 6ᵀᴴ, 1923

THE PHILOSOPHY OF HUNTING CLOTHES

BY MAX BAKER

The rules of "no brown in town" should evidently always be applied – and sportsmen should, it seems, take more care in their appearance.

THE WELL-TURNED-OUT participator in some sporting functions may succeed in conveying the impression that his *tout ensemble* is no more than a happy accident, dictated no doubt by a desire to be inconspicuous, but question him tactfully and you will discover that he really takes an interest in getting everything just right. Others, with fewer views of their own trust to their tailor and at times unduly reflect the idiosyncrasies of one whose enthusiasm for what he imagines to be style may outrun the limits of good taste. A lady whom I induced to discuss the subject frankly, asked which in my opinion was worse, the man of town associations who had dressed for a country function or the country dweller who essayed a town appearance with corresponding lack of knowledge. And yet the most remarkable aspect of any fortuitous gathering of sportsmen is their seeming indifference to set style, always combined with a rightness in their variety which no doubt results from experience. When present at a recent event connected with shooting I amused myself by examining certain costumes which were present and was amazed to discover that only one tailor seemed to have hit off a perfect representation of "plus four" knickerbockers. In the others the concertina effect was present to a greater or less degree, but, happily there was no example of the pair

> "ONLY ONE TAILOR SEEMS TO HAVE HIT OFF A PERFECT REPRESENTATION OF 'PLUS FOUR' KNICKERBOCKERS"

of loose-hanging sacks which is perhaps the least pleasing of the several extremes into which this difficult garment is apt to roam.

As regards coats, I have found that there are two distinct schools among the tailoring fraternity – those who think that ease of movement is given by bagginess and large armholes and the others who affirm that since the tightest military tunic affords unexpected freedom to the arms, therefore, the arm holes should be shaped close up to the socket of the shoulder and freedom be given solely by skilful fitting. The last are undoubtedly right and that is perhaps why the simple lounge coat has proved itself the next easiest garment to the jersey or its equivalent. The subject bristles with interest and I should like to see it discussed knowledgeably with references to practical examples such as I have taken the liberty of borrowing from real life.

NOVEMBER 3ᴿᴰ, 1950

SHOOTING CLOTHES

BY MacDONALD HASTINGS

THE EMINENT VICTORIAN sportsman who devised a shooting hat made out of a dead hedgehog made, I suppose, the most memorable attempt to resolve a problem which has baffled countrymen since the invention of gunpowder. The right clothes for a shooting party are still anybody's fancy. So much so that I shall never be surprised if, instead of a sweepstake on the bag, the ladies are invited to award prizes for the best fancy dress.

In theory, there is a convention that people who go shooting wear tweed knickerbocker suits (not too baggy) in dark shades, with a cap to match, and a mackintosh. But I never seem to meet those types outside the advertisements. My own impression of a typical shooting party, shown Stands 1 to 8, is more like this:

No. 1 – The Week-ender. Newmarket boots, check riding breeches, deerstalker hat, and a full-skirted dun-coloured coat which looks as if it were made by sewing a lot of pockets together.

No. 2 – The Crack Shot. Gum boots and plus fours worn underneath oilskin over trouser. A sort of battledress coat and a fisherman's hat.

No. 3 – The Dandy. Skin-tight tweed knickers, white spats and porpoise-hide boots. Norfolk jacket with flaps on all pockets. Green snap-brimmed slouch hat.

No. 4 – The Farmer. Pigskin leggings and breeches, hacking jacket and cap, old gas mask bag across shoulder.

No. 5 – The Eccentric. White stockings and Scottish brogues with black ankle-laces. Khaki shorts, high-necked sweater, and naval duffle-coat with hood.

No. 6 – The Fellow Who Borrows One of Your Guns. Corduroy slacks, open-necked shirt, twill coat and town shoes.

No. 7 – The Weather Prophet. Fishing waders, unspeakably aged tweed suit, oilskin hat, and a roll of waterproof on back.

No. 8 – The Youngster. Jodhpurs and gum-boots, silk scarf, tweed jacket – and no mackintosh when it rains.

If you want to raise a laugh about clothes at a shooting lunch, the only safe bet is to describe the ridiculous appearance of Continental sportsmen, who are said to have tassels on their cartridge bags, or the Americans, who wear red peaked caps and dress up for shooting like baseball players. But they haven't our climate to contend with.

DECEMBER 10TH, 1921

SHOOTING NOTES: A NOVEL FORM OF PULL-THROUGH

BY MAX BAKER

A novel and simple way of cleaning the barrels of your shotgun that can be completed in ten seconds flat.

I ONCE MADE rather a quaint variation of the ordinary shotgun pull-through prove an extremely useful addition to the equipment of every gunroom. Its principal feature is an old muzzle-loading rod, incidentally the only one I have ever seen made of bamboo. A little alteration to the ferrule enabled it to receive and retain a knotted cord. The free end of the cord was spliced to form a lassoo loop, through which a rag of appropriate size was drawn. The contrivance, as illustrated, can be dropped down the barrel without any of the niggling delay due to feeding the weight of an ordinary pull-through, and it can be drawn out from the muzzle end at express speed. Ten seconds is the timed period of pulling it through the barrels. After that a rod fitted with the stiff bristle brush requires to be vigorously worked up and down inside, so scrubbing out any adhering fouling and even taking away leading not too intimately amalgamated with the bore surface.

An open bath of oil is necessary for conveniently applying the cleansing agent, and nothing is better for the purpose than one of the squat ink bottles which are fitted with a hinged lid. The cleaning brush should not be dipped in the oil, but a round artist's brush, size No. 10, be used as conveyor. This same brush serves for anointing the inmost recesses of metal surfaces as a preliminary to vigorous rag rubbing. A great advantage of the rod form of pull-through is that one naturally stands it up in a corner, the rag being thus saved from its inherent tendency to gather grit and other filth. I have often wondered why the gun trade has devoted so little attention to the provision of these gunroom conveniences, for their effort ceases when the portable outfit, as stowed in the guncase, has been made up. Lately I approached one of my friends in the trade on the subject, and he promised to experiment in the direction indicated. I shall give the enterprise all the encouragement possible, but promise to stand clear of any commercial results that may accrue.

ETIQUETTE IN COVERT SHOOTING

Shooting another man's bird is bad form, but so is wasting an opportunity – a correspondent lays down some guidelines.

TO THE EDITOR OF "COUNTRY LIFE."

SIR,—Shooting, as I happen to do, in many different parts of England and Scotland, it is amusing to see how very different locally is the etiquette in covert shooting about taking your neighbour's bird, or shooting in the tail that bird that might have given another gun a shot at its head. The highest perfection of courtesy we find, I think, in the great shooting counties, notably Norfolk, where a man going with the beaters would no more think of shooting a bird, even though he were a high and good bird, going forward to the heading guns than the French, on a certain historical occasion, could think of firing before the English. As for shooting what is obviously another man's bird, it happens so rarely that I think we are justified in saying that "it is not done." It is also as contrary to the etiquette to fire a long or doubtful shot. A new guest thus offending is not likely to be asked again. If you go more into the Midlands, or in what are called the Home Counties, you will find much less formality. There is a disposition, not confessed in so many words, to shoot where there is a chance. If a man shoots another's bird he apologises indeed, but thinks that by the apology he has more than covered an offence which, committed in Norfolk, would have made him wish to sink into the ground for shame. But still long shots are not the rule but the exception. The rule as to the heading guns taking *all* the birds that go forward is less

> "THE HIGHEST PERFECTION OF COURTESY WE FIND, I THINK, IN THE GREAT SHOOTING COUNTIES"

severe. Passing on from these to the mountainous counties, Devonshire, Wales, parts of Scotland, and so on, the "grand manner" is banished nearly altogether. True, one does not seek to shoot another's bird, but if one so does, by accident, all there is to say is "Oh, well, I had to shoot when I got the chance," and that closes the incident, and gives a key to the whole difference in etiquette.—UBIQUE

WILD FOWLING IN WAR-TIME

BY J. WENTWORTH DAY

James Wentworth Day was one of the most famous wildfowlers of his time – as well as being a broadcaster and author on many subjects, including farming and ghost hunting.

[Stringent war-time restrictions are imposed by the Admiralty and local military authorities on punt-gunners and coastal wild-fowlers. Permits to shoot are granted only to responsible persons, and shooting is only allowed between dawn and dusk. The courage and endurance of some of the men who supply the London market today with their stick of wild geese and duck are here described by Mr. Wentworth Day who has had long experience of wild-fowling.—Ed]

WE SAILED UNDER an admiralty permit towards that enchanted isle where, in summer, shell-duck and redshank nest and in winter the black-geese sit on the sand-bar, croaking in their thousands. We sailed in the smack *Joseph and Mary*, blessed be her holy memories, carrying two single punts of the open Essex sort, clinker-built, with two muzzle-loading guns, the first, Roaring Tom, which weighs a hundred and ten pounds and fires a pound and a quarter of shot, and the second, the Tiddley Bit of "The Little Owd Half-Pounder."

In the tiny cabin, twelve-feet by six by four-feet-six – we sleep two in one bunk, head and toe, one in the other and two on the floor, feet to the stove – we got out the kettle and frying-pan, fried dabs and little soles, made hot black tea, ate cold widgeon with our fingers, spread the hot fish on thick bread and talked of these war hazards which send duck and geese to the London markets.

The world was a place of ghostly mists and clawing frosts. The tide stole landward, silky and gurgling. Bar-geese laughed in the fog. The fishermen will tell you that they are the voices of drowned sailors mocking on the tide line at those who are about to follow. High up the creek came the muffled cronking of Brent Geese, the "Wheoh" and purr of widgeon, the hoarse quack of mallard. "They're a-singin' out on the mud all right – we'll warm 'em." The two punts slide overboard without a splash. The guns were lowered, breeched and trimmed.

"Br–r–r–oomp–oomp–oomp!" Twin reports and twin tongues of flame flashed and thundered almost as one. He had pulled his lanyard as they sat, as his boot toe thumped down. Mine was pulled as they jumped. We cut a double lane through them. And as the skirl of voices, the tornado of wings filled the upper air in a sudden frenzy, we punted rapidly on the mud bank, 12-bores banging right and left at the cripples.

Over all this was the wild whistle of widgeon, the shriek of curlew, the distant thunder of geese rising in their thousands from far-off mud banks, the sonorous squawk of a flurried heron, the lap of the memorial tide. Thirty-six geese and widgeon, a pair of mallard and a grey plover, a mixed bag to feed many human mouths.

> ## "THE WORLD WAS A PLACE OF GHOSTLY MISTS AND CLAWING FROSTS"

AUGUST 28ᵀᴴ, 1942

SHOOTING CROWS WITH AN OWL DECOY

BY COUNT BJORN VON ROSEN

SHOOTING CROWS WITH a horned owl as a decoy is a Swedish sport that is both amusing and provocative of thought. It is most profitable in March and October, during the spring and autumn flights; the weather should be warm for the time of year, cloudy and absolutely calm.

You must be at the hide soon after dawn, the owl is carried in the traditional manner under your arm, wrapped in a sack so that his feet (one of them being equipped with a leather lead and ring with which to manoeuvre him) and sticking forward conspicuously, and held firmly so that they may be watched while you walk. Make no mistake about his claws; our keeper was very careless on one occasion, perhaps a bit slack in his hold after ten years uneventful handling of the owl, and in consequence had to be taken to hospital for treatment to his thigh, where the owl's claws had gone in so deeply that, as he said, they "met in the bone."

"Kraah, kraah!" The crow is still a bit cautious and suspicious; perhaps he is a local crow who has seen the owl-hide before in

the spring. The owl follows the circling with his eyes gazing upwards as though he would transfix him with frigid piercing pupils. Wherever he circles, the owl turns his head; otherwise he sits absolutely still. Involuntarily you wait for the slight crack when one of the bones in his neck should snap, but it never comes; when his head is nearly three-quarters round, he turns it back and stares from the other side.

More voices become detached from the grey dawning sky. A small flock of three or four have arrived, drawn out of the sky by their solitary forerunner. Still more come; the uproar increases, one pitches in the birch in front of the opening of the hide, but you still hold your fire. Suddenly the air round the hide grows black as a large flock is swept downwards out of the sky, a robber band of 40 or 50 furiously clamorous, filling the neighbourhood with an indescribable tumult.

The frenzy is at boiling point; the boldest among the newcomers makes violent downward thrusts towards the owl, who draws up his large wings to shield himself, glancing out under the joints with his consistently expressionless gloomy stare; sometimes he cowers a bit when the most insolent one whistles along a few inches above his tufted ears. All the time some crow or another is sitting in the birch, swaying, bowing, and dancing and producing the loudest expression of fury; occasionally three or four perch on the same branch. You wait until you get two of them fairly well in line, and fire.

JULY 29TH, 1922

CROCODILE SHOOTING

To the Editor of "Country Life."

Sir,—There are two places in Uganda that I know of as being specially patronised by the crocodile. The first place is just a few miles westward of Entebbe on Lake Victoria, where the shore is rocky and small rocky islands abound. Here the reptiles simply swarm, and as they are aroused from their sleep on the rocks by the approaching canoe it appears as if the whole surface of the rock is sliding in water. The second favourite haunt of the reptile is the first reach of the Nile for twenty miles from its source, where the accompanying photograph was taken. Crocodiles at the Ripon Falls (the source of the Nile) were the subjects of many legends, and the traveller on the Lake steamers always took his rifle for a shot at them while the steamer was in port at Jiuja. The shooting is quite good sport. One can sit on the bank and fire at them crossing the river. As only the tip of the nose is showing while the crocodile is swimming, fine shooting is necessary. This, however, is rather unsatisfactory, for whether a hit is made or not, the beast disappears under the water. If killed, the body is swiftly carried away by the current, so one is always uncertain of the result.

"NO COMPUNCTION NEED BE FELT IN SHOOTING THE CROCODILE"

The most interesting sport is obtained by shooting at the sleeping reptile on a rock. Approach to nearer than 100 yds. is almost impossible, for the crocodile is either keen of hearing or of scent. The only vital spot to hit is the eye, or very near it (a bullet will rarely enter the horny hide), and as the beast lies flat on a rock, which it greatly resembles in colour, it has a good sporting chance of escape, unless the marksman is more than ordinarily expert. Field-glasses are often necessary. No compunction need be felt in shooting the crocodile, for where so numerous it is a constant worry to the natives.—E. Brown

SEPTEMBER 23ᴿᴰ, 1899

GROUSE SHOOTING OVER DOGS

A sport unique to the British Isles, grouse shooting is considered to be the best and most challenging of all game shooting, especially when the pleasure of watching dogs work is added.

WE MUST ALWAYS deem the grouse shooting the best of all, not only because it really is the best, the wildest, the most beautiful, but also because it is the first; because we begin to shoot the grouse earlier in the year than the date at which we may begin the shooting of our less interesting partridges and pheasants. It is not with any notion of belittling the merits of either of these Southern game birds that we give this prize to the grouse.

There is always a special interest, too, in seeing to what extent the summer holidays have interrupted the course of the dogs' breaking. It is seldom that even the most trustworthy will begin a new season with all the caution and wisdom that he had learned at the conclusion of the last. It is not in canine nature that he should. And if this occasion of the first point is an exciting one for the dog, it is scarcely less exciting for the shooter too. There is always a certain nervous tremor as the moment approaches for THE FIRST SHOT OF THE SEASON, a certain feeling of relief when this first shot is over, and a sense of satisfaction as of a good omen

(even for the least superstitious of us) if this first shot be well executed. No less so does it seem to augur ill if this first shot be a miss.

There are some men, and some good shots, who assert roundly that they do not care to see the dogs work, it gives them no pleasure, they take no interest in it. Of them we can only say that to lose so considerable source of satisfaction argues a most unfortunate disposition or a very crass stupidity. There is a glory of driving, and there is a glory of shooting over dogs; but to deny all glory, as some are inclined to deny it, to the one does not in the least enhance the glory of the other. Thackeray once rebuked a young man who complained of having had a bad dinner in immortal words: "No dinner is bad, some are better than others" So, too, no grouse shooting is bad, though some grouse shooting may be better than others.

MAY 19TH, 1900

A LITTLE INVENTION

An early hand-held clay trap is proposed by a Country Life *correspondent.*

TO THE EDITOR OF "COUNTRY LIFE."

SIR,—I have just had a chance of inspecting a little invention that will be of the utmost use to shooters. It is practically a wooden and metal sling for throwing claybirds. There seems to be no doubt about it that it will, by its convenience, hit the orthodox traps very hard. It throws with even more power than the traps – or than most of them, does not break the birds, and any country boy who can throw a stone is able to send rocketers off the top of a hay rick, or from the other side of it, such as will try the skill of even quick game shots.—ARGUS OLIVE

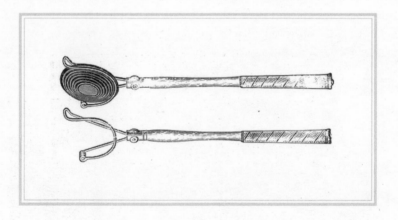

DECEMBER 11TH, 1909

SHOOTING AT SANDRINGHAM

THE KING HAD king's weather for the celebration of his birthday at Sandringham this year, and in characteristic style it was celebrated by a shooting party in which the King himself, the Prince of Wales, the Duke of Teck and a number of visitors at Sandringham took part. On the first day they proceeded to the Anmer and Sherbourne fields for partridge shooting; but, unfortunately, the excellent sport they enjoyed was marred by the sudden death of Mr. Montague Guest, who dropped dead in a field.

There is no property in Norfolk more favoured than that of Sandringham, where the photograph was taken and, by gracious permission, we are allowed to reproduce. Both the ordinary covert shooting and also the partridge shooting are of the best. Possibly the best covert of all the ground is Wolferton Wood, which runs beside the road from Dersingham to King's Lynn. It appears to be a tradition, though not invariably observed, that it should be shot on December 1st, the present Queen's birthday.

MAY 23RD, 1925

KILLING PARTRIDGES WITH A TENNIS RACKET

An account of an unconventional and rather unsporting way of catching a brace of partridge.

TO THE EDITOR OF "COUNTRY LIFE."

SIR,—Many implements and instruments have been put to strange uses for which they were not intended, but it is not often that a tennis racket has taken the place of a gun to kill partridges! During my wanderings in Rhodesia, it was my lot on one evening to be stationed on a particularly lonely outpost – the total number of Europeans numbered six. It was my custom in hot weather to have my evening meal on the verandah. One evening a very heavy thunderstorm came down, and like most tropical storms, was over inside an hour. After the downpour the table was laid as usual, with a paraffin lamp in the centre, and I sat down to my lonely meal. But I was not to be left undisturbed. Myriads of huge flying ants invaded my quarters, attracted by the light, and in no time the table was

covered with these insects, falling into the soup, into the butter, into everything. Knowing it was the light that attracted them, I went inside and ate my meal in comparative darkness. Shortly after I stepped out into the light to see how the ants were enjoying themselves, when, to my surprise, I saw a "swempe" (native name for partridge), unconcernedly enjoying a meal off them. Quickly backing into the room, my eyes fell on my tennis racket, the only article I thought would be of any use. Cautiously I slipped out, and before the astonished partridge could fly away I banged it up against the corrugated iron walls of the hut – dead. As the insects were still there in their numbers I went back into the hut and lay down on my bed. About half an hour after I came out, and to my utter astonishment another partridge – probably the mate – was on the verandah catching the insects as fast as he could! Backing once more into the hut I took hold of the racket and while it was looking in the opposite direction, I made a sudden dash, and before the bird could fly off, a swift blow ended its life. My next day's meal was assured in the shape of two fine "swempe" without a shot having been fired in obtaining it.—H. D. LONGDEN

JANUARY 20TH, 1912

THE KING-EMPEROR SHOOTING IN NEPAL

PHOTOGRAPHY HAS ACHIEVED a great triumph in bringing before us so vividly the picturesque conditions under which sport is conducted in the State of Nepal. This week we are enabled to show photographs of the actual sport enjoyed by the King. One or two features are so obvious that they will scarcely escape the attention of any reader. The first is the conspicuous part played by the elephant. This animal is nearly as important in the actual chase as the hunter who rides on his back. He has been trained from infancy, and probably has inherited certain attributes that make for usefulness from progenitors who were employed in the same way.

"THE KING APPEARS TO BE IMPERVIOUS TO PHYSICAL FEAR"

The King, like all the other members of the Royal Family, appears to be impervious to physical fear. He shot as coolly and well as though he had been in one of the pheasant preserves at Sandringham.

OCTOBER 27TH, 1900

HIS FIRST HERON

To the Editor of "Country Life."

Sir,—I enclose a photograph which you may deem suitable for insertion in your paper. It was sent me by a nephew who wrote as follows: "I send you a photograph of my first heron. I stalked it along the shore at Innellan, and got within 200 yds. before shooting it with my small rifle. Sheila photographed us both next morning, and I think she did her work very well. Unfortunately it was a young bird, and its plume was not fully grown, so I did not have it stuffed." I need not say I gave the "young barbarian" a good lecture on the useless slaughter of a beautiful bird.—R. G.

FISHING

In its pages devoted to the art of fishing, Country Life not only covers the craft of tying knots and spinning baits, but also why the fisherman should never allow his wife to accompany him to the riverbank.

❖ VII ❖

THE OFFICES OF
"COUNTRY LIFE"
LONDON
THE OFFICES OF
"COUNTRY LIFE"

SEPTEMBER 27TH, 1946

THE ETIQUETTE OF FISHING

BY ROY BEDDINGTON

A good explanation for why fishing is a solitary sport.

"THERE IS ALWAYS a best way of doing everything, if it be to boil an egg. Manners are the happy ways of doing things." Emerson's words apply to fishing, as to all worldly pursuits.

Do not arrive at the water with your wife, children, dog or camp followers without asking if they can come. Some are well trained, suitably clothed and wise to the ways of fishermen; others are not. From the uninitiated I have suffered. On one occasion a fellow to whom I had given permission to fish brought in his train a lady, uninvited and attired as for the Lido. She had no interest in fishing, as was soon apparent, for she spent the morning picking primulas and iris in the water garden and the afternoon, since the day was hot and she had very few clothes to remove, bathing in the best pool on the water where I had elected to fish. Such visitors are not asked twice; they pay a price for the bad manners of

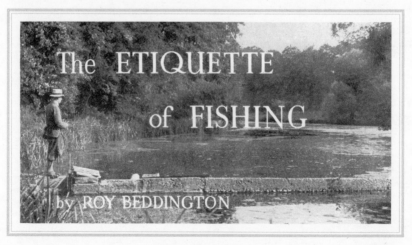

those whom they bring. Those who ask blatantly for fishing and when permission is given take all for granted, seldom receive a second invitation.

There is the man who, as soon as he sees another fishing on the opposite bank, hurries to arrive at the best stretch before him. It is so easy to accost the other in a friendly fashion with a remark such as "Shall I be in your way here?" or "If you would like to fish that bit I will start in two or three hundred yards above." Such an overture is a sign of good manners. If you fix up a plan at the beginning with your adversary, as some like to call him, you will have a much pleasanter day than if you are jockeying for position from morning to night.

"DO NOT ARRIVE AT THE WATER WITH YOUR WIFE, CHILDREN, DOG OR CAMP FOLLOWERS WITHOUT ASKING IF THEY CAN COME"

Do not recount your experiences at length to others unless they ask for them. Otherwise you will become a bore; and it is well to remember that the haunt of such creatures is not only the best armchair at the club.

THE PLEASANT CURIOSITY OF FISH AND FISHING: THE TROUT THAT SUCCEEDED...

[Scene: A moorland pass high up under heather ridges in the West Country. A trout stream brawls amongst great concourse of boulders spread down the coomb; high hills tower upon either hand; and through the desolation pass Mr. and Mrs. Frank Trevor. 'Tis their honeymoon; but thunder broods in the upper chambers of the air, and relations are somewhat strained, for Trevor has been fishing three hours and caught nothing.]

He *(on one side of the river)*: Come over here, and let us eat our lunch. *(Flings himself down in the shadow of a great rock and opens his creel.)*

She *(on the other side)*: I can't get across, Frank.

He: Oh, yes you can. It's all right. Jump and chance it. You can take the wretched stream in your stride down there.

She *(arriving hot and disappointed that he would not help her as usual)*: I nearly twisted my ankle –

He: What's that forsaken-looking thing done up at the bottom of my creel?

She: I slipped it in there – it's the duck we didn't eat last night.

He: Why on earth didn't you say so before? Here I've been choking myself with these infernal sandwiches and a cold duck under my nose!

She: I forgot it.

He: You'll have to pay a little more attention to detail, Maude, when we go home. I'm not a difficult man to please, and, as you know, eating and drinking are the last things I care about, but hang it – oh, d— the flies, they're on everything!

She *(resenting his threat)*: Funny with so many flies about that you can't catch a trout. They eat flies, don't they?

He: Trout! I'm sick of the name of trout, and sick of the lies they tell about fishing at the farm. There's always some wretched doctor, or postman, or ploughboy, who's just caught three dozen, or killed a two-pounder, or some rot of that sort. Whereas the truth is there aren't any trout worth mentioning between here and the Midlands. Dartmoor's all right, no doubt, if you happen to be a convict in want of five years' penal servitude; and that's about the only thing it's good for, apparently. From the point of view of sport, it's enough to turn a man's hair grey.

"WELL JUMPED! THERE, LIGHT AS A FEATHER."

FISHING IN MONTENEGRO

A correspondent describes the rather eccentric mode of fishing employed in Montenegro.

To the Editor of "Country Life."

Sir,—I enclose a photograph of Montenegrins shooting fish. This sport is by no means easy, though it is facilitated to some extent by the fact that a bullet passing near to a fish will often stun it by its sudden impact on hitting the water.—Harry McIlroy, H.M.S. *Dublin*

FISHING WITH A GLASS-
BOTTOMED BOX

TO THE EDITOR OF "COUNTRY LIFE."

SIR,—I am sending you a photograph of a form of fishing practised in Japan which might have its votaries at health resorts in England as a means of passing the time and a variation of shrimping. With the help of a glass fixed into a box, this Japanese fisherman can see distinctly what is swimming underneath him, and kill the fish with a spear which he carries in his other hand.—D. C.

DECEMBER 31ST, 1921

SOME DEFECTS IN SPINNING PIKE BAITS AND WAYS OF REMEDYING THEM

BY CLARENCE PONTING

WHEN ONE THINKS of the improvements which have been made in the accessories used by sportsmen during the past forty years, it seems a remarkable thing that fishing has practically stood still as far as spinning baits are concerned. The same designs are being used today, some cases under the same names as those which were described and illustrated in the piscatorial books of 1881.

> "WHO SHALL SAY WHAT SIZE OUR FISH BAITS SHOULD BE?"

This cannot be due to perfection in design, because, as every practical pike fisher knows, the perfect spinner has yet to be invented.

The correct size of a spinning bait is really difficult to determine, because the larger and more weighty the lure, the more difficult is it to spin. Three inches is quite large enough to spin comfortably, and if made of brass or German silver is sufficiently heavy to enable the angler to dispense with weights on the gimp or running line. But at the same time it suffers from the disadvantage that quite small pike or perch can take it. In the summer I hooked and landed one which was very little bigger than the bait. When fish of this size will persist in running at the lure, who shall say what size our fish baits should be?

INSTRUCTIONS FOR MAKING CORKSCREW BAIT.

For a 3in. bait, cut head of spinner as shown in the diagram, 1¼in. by 1¼in. Then cut out flat strip of tin 6ins. long by ¾in. or 1in. wide, rounding the broad portion and bringing the other end nearly to a

point. Then solder the head of bait on to the broad portion at about the angle in the illustration. If soldered in line with flat tin strip, the head will not come straight with the bait when rolled. Next roll the flat tin strip spirally round a thin pencil,

leaving a gap or space between the tin edges of about ⅛in. Obtain a piece of hard brass wire 2mm. in thickness and 4ins. long. Turn the ends into loops with a pair of round-nosed pliers after moulding ½ oz. or ¾ oz. of lead on the centre.

Then solder this wire strongly at the head and tail ends of the bait. Attach a small split ring to each loop to take a

swivel at head and a triangle hook at end, covering the hooks with scarlet floss or worsted. A second hook can be attached on the wire near the head if desired.

The lead is moulded on to the wire by taking a tin of sifted sand made slightly damp. In the centre of the sand push down the tapered end of a penholder to the depth of about 1½ins. Then push the wire into the sand, which will hold the wire upright in the middle of the mould. Then pour in the molten lead which

will be more or less wedge-shaped and file into a tapering point at the thick end. The triple hook on tail must be free to swing easily or the bait will not spin.

Another bait which I have made is "The Corkscrew".

AUGUST 29TH, 1941

THE FISHERMAN'S CURSE

BY ROY BEDDINGTON

THE FISHERMAN, IF happy, is, it seems, afflicted with curses other than that which under the title "Fisherman's curse!" already has a twofold meaning. Piscatorially the "Fisherman's Curse" signifies a minute insect of the *diptera* family, upon which trout are wont, upon occasion, to feed, to the annoyance of the angler who is supposed to voice his exasperation with curses. The phrase, used botanically, is a term for the water fig wort, which is said to call forth like oaths from the angler whose cast has become entangled in its withered capsules. But these are small discomforts compared with those other curses which hover above the fisherman's head and bring down upon it a multitude of woes, disappointments, and discontent.

"THERE IS HASTY JUDGEMENT, LACK OF PATIENCE, AN AFFINITY FOR WORMS OR PRAWNS – ALL PRESENTS FROM THE DEVIL…"

Bulls drive the fisher to the security of upper branches, while cows eat his lunch (or his paraphernalia). Coots and moorhens disturb the water at his coming. Water rats undermine his banks. Tame ducks swim back and forth to cause annoyance, while the female mallard flaps the water as she feigns a broken wing. He is provoked to curse. Perhaps he who curses is himself cursed.

There are the fisherman's personal afflictions. There is forgetfulness, which vice he shares with the plumber (the slipping water must affect the memory of both). The curse of forgotten tools is cast upon them. Reel or pipe, casts of fly-box left behind can upset the fisherman's sport. There is bad eyesight and spectacles that fall into the water, when the rise is on. There is hasty judgement, lack of patience, an affinity for worms or prawns – all presents from the devil – to curse.

Today the fisherman cut off from his river by the fortunes of war, needs something to take his imagination to pleasant waters and cause him to wield an imaginary rod.

DECEMBER 4TH, 1942

FISHING WITH DYNAMITE

BY T. C. BRIDGES

An extraordinary account of German bombers providing a feast of fish during World War II.

I WAS STANDING on a cliff top in a south-west coast town when two German aeroplanes came over in a desperate hurry. One jettisoned two bombs as it scudded out to sea. The first bomb fell in the harbour, the second just outside. I had my field glasses and when the commotion had subsided I focused them on the spot. I was surprised at the number of fish which floated on the surface. There must have been several hundred.

> "ONCE I SAW WHAT A STICK OF DYNAMITE COULD DO TO A RIVER POOL"

Once I saw what a stick of dynamite could do to a river pool. With a friend I was walking home on a September evening after a day's ferreting when I heard a dull thud in the distance. It came from a wooded stretch of the Dart. We ran for the spot. I suppose we made a good deal of noise bursting through the bushes, for when we reached the bank we saw two men bolting up the opposite hill. There was no means of crossing and we did not recognise the men. Scores of dead fish floated on the surface. I would not have believed there could have been so many in a comparatively small though deep pool. Most were small brown trout, but there were several peal up to 3 lb. in weight. With a long-handled landing net we could have filled a small sack. We did not wait but hurried down to the bailiff. He was fairly sure of the identity of the fish killers but of course he had no proof.

Fishing with dynamite is still a too usual practice in America and Australia. Some years ago Mr. Stratford Jolly took part in some search for the famous treasure of the Square Stone, supposed to be hidden in the heart of the Bolivian hills. When the search failed he and another of the party decided to travel northwards to the Amazon by way of the little known Urubamda river. After many adventures food ran out; there was no game and they nearly starved. Luckily they had dynamite. A stick of it was tied to a stone and a very short fuse attached. The explosion brought several fish to the surface, including one resembling a salmon, which weighed 20 lb. and proved to be excellent eating. So for once fishing with dynamite was justified.

OCTOBER 1ST, 1921

THE PRIME MINISTER IN THE WESTERN HIGHLANDS

David Lloyd George takes a fishing holiday in Scotland.

TO THE EDITOR OF "COUNTRY LIFE."

SIR,—I hope you may like to see these two photographs of the Prime Minister and his family rejoicing over his first salmon. Incidentally may I point out a slip in your note on his visit to Scotland in last week's issue? You say that "the Glasgow people have always regarded the Gairloch as the supreme holiday attraction," but the place loved by Glasgow is in Argyllshire, the Western arm of Loch Fyne, and is spelt Gareloch. It is some way from Gairloch in Ross and Cromarty where the Prime Minister has been staying.—LOCH MAREE

JULY 15TH, 1939

A FISHERMAN'S DIARY – *PECHE ARDENNAISE*

THE WATER EXHIBITION at Liège – a most excellent effort on the part of the Belgian Government – prompts me to write of a day's fishing which I had last autumn in the Ardennes. The river – a limestone stream about the size of the Dorset Frome – curves this way and that between long lines of poplars. Our rendezvous was the old mill, where Monsieur Poligne, his wife, and his two sons, were waiting to greet us with information of a large trout hooked and lost in the *bief* – the mill leet.

The gentlemen of the *Amicale* were thick upon the banks, since it was the last day of the season. Some with ordinary fly rods, others with spinning rods or huge bamboo poles – eighteen to twenty feet at least in length, with a bunch of worms at the end. The river abounds with trout, grayling, chubb, eels, and a few pike.

I put up my rod and was taken off to fish in the *bief*, a beautiful piece of water – more enjoyable, since it provided welcome respite from the bamboos and minnows the owners of which think nothing of fishing across the line of the unfortunate fellow on the other side.

Here were trout in plenty; but it was so bright, with an east wind and its accompanying haze, that chances of success were poor. However, I saw a fish rise and, after much trouble with overhanging branches, as the trees and bushes had not been cut, succeeded in rising him; but I struck too quickly, and the fly, as flies are wont to do on such occasions, stuck fast in the upper branches of a tall poplar behind me.

We took down our rods at the mill and walked back to our inn in the village. The sky was purple and gold, and against it was the deep blue silhouette of the church and its cluster of houses, looking like a hen and her brood of chicks.—ROY BEDDINGTON

JULY 15TH, 1939

EXPERIMENTS WITH FISHING GUT

A bit of practical advice on how to tie a knot properly.

NEW KNOTS WERE invented, lubricants, adhesives, and solvents used all to no purpose. Chator's remained the best, the only snag being that for twenty years I had found it difficult to tie, with certainty, twice alike. Again there was a simple explanation. It has fifteen practicable variations.

It is tied with ease and rapidity even in the dusk, thus: *soak the gut.* Hold the two strands between the left thumb and forefinger. Keep them well separated and parallel. Do not cross them. Short end at the bottom, the long one at the top. Thumbnail should be vertical. Twist the short around the long over and away for three full turns and then over again and back towards between the separated strands as they emerge from the finger grip. Now grasp the lot between the thumb and forefinger of the right hand. See that the end is secured and that the strands remain well separated. Twist up the left side of the knot with the left hand still maintaining the same direction of rotation. Three full turns and then tuck the end under and away between the strands at the grip. The left side always seems to have an extra half-turn, but this is only because rotation commenced with the top instead of the bottom strand. Release the grip and pull up steadily and firmly by the long ends. Saliva as a lubricant is good for the final pull. Until a better knot is found, it seems folly ever again to describe in a book any knot for joining two strands, except the double blood.

After several years of intermittent work with the Ballistic Tester these conclusions have been reached. All knots are bad, but the best for joining gut is Chator's double blood. For fine gut, three and three-quarter turns

"ALL KNOTS ARE BAD"

reverse twist, symmetrical, ends protruding on opposite sides, that is, right half, three and back; left half, three and away, left half three and back. There is a falling-off in strength above and below these limits.

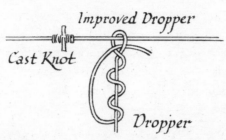

METHOD OF ATTACHING DROPPER

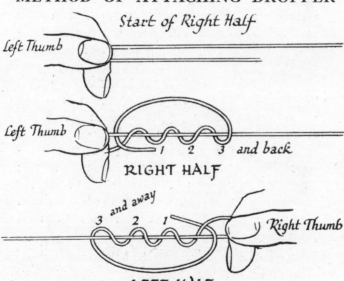

CHATOR'S DOUBLE BLOOD KNOT
3¾ turns reverse twist, symmetrical, ends protruding on opposite sides

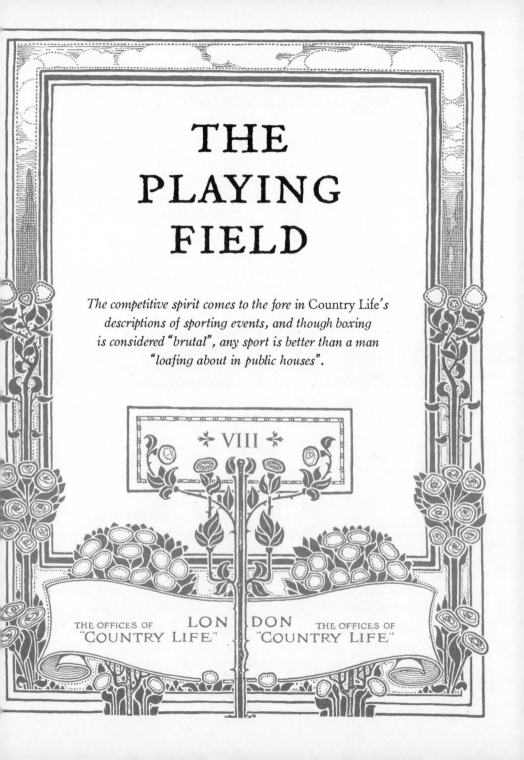

THE
PLAYING
FIELD

*The competitive spirit comes to the fore in Country Life's
descriptions of sporting events, and though boxing
is considered "brutal", any sport is better than a man
"loafing about in public houses".*

❧ VIII ❧

THE OFFICES OF   LONDON   THE OFFICES OF
"COUNTRY LIFE"   "COUNTRY LIFE"

JULY 9ᵀᴴ, 1901

OUR MANLY AMUSEMENTS

ONE OF OUR contemporaries reminds us that it is just 200 years since the birth of John Broughton, who was called the "Father of English Boxing." He strayed accidentally as it were into the paths of pugilism, having made discovery of his own prowess through having to fight with a fellow-workman. So satisfied was he with the result that he began to challenge people to fight him for wagers, and this laid the foundation of the profession of boxing, which counted so much to our ancestors of the eighteenth and early part of the nineteenth centuries.

Looking back, we are sometimes tempted to regard the vigorous generation that encouraged prize-fighting as being somewhat brutal in character, and indeed the amusements that were carried on simultaneously with this one could scarcely be called refined. Cocking was then in great favour, although it did not reach its zenith till after the battle of Waterloo, when a great main was fought, in which the birds were named respectively after the English and the French generals who were in command on that occasion. The cock-pit was then a most popular institution. So in a lesser degree was the rat-pit, and the tiny black and tan terrier that would kill its own weight in rats in as many minutes as it weighed pounds was held to be a treasure among dogs. Badger-baiting was also a common amusement.

It might be seriously asked if we really have improved much on those brutal pastimes. Again, for boxing at the present moment wrestling has been largely substituted, and here, again, we do not know that much improvement is to be noticed.

For the sake of the country it is much to be desired that means may be found of popularising the old sports without making them into so many hunting-grounds for the professional. But though the attraction possessed by the sports we have referred to shows that the old Adam still exists in the British public, it is pleasant to remember that our amusements have been very much improved during the past twenty or thirty years. Golf, motoring, football, cricket are all outdoor pastimes which take one into the fresh air and improve both mind and body, while the bicycle provides exercise for thousands who in former days used to spend their leisure in loafing about public-houses.

JULY 12ᵀᴴ, 1919

THE LAWN TENNIS CHAMPIONSHIPS

BY F. R. BURROW

Wimbledon has been held since 1877, making it the oldest tennis tournament in the world.

WHETHER THE "VICTORY" Championships will go down to history as "The Wet Wimbledon" or "The Wonderful Wimbledon" time alone can tell. On the whole, I think, the latter is the likelier; for although rain played an almost unprecedented part in prolonging the meeting, there were yet features of the play which caused the thronged stands to forget all past delays and disappointments in present enthusiasm and excitement.

" 'THE WET WIMBLEDON' OR 'THE WONDERFUL WIMBLEDON' "

The Championships of 1919 differed from the great majority of their predecessors in that the winner of both the All Comers' Singles were almost taken for granted. This might seem to militate against excitement; but then – there are the challenge rounds! At Wimbledon the holders "stand out," awaiting, with what calmness they can command, the surviving hero or heroine, from the long lists of the world's best players. Thus, splendidly isolated, they have every opportunity of studying the strokes and tactics of those who will at long last throw down the gauntlet to them in the Centre Court – that hallowed enclosure where every good player hopes to appear at least once before his game passes from him.

The questions, then, which were asked this year were not "Who will win the All Comers?" but "Will Patterson beat Brookes?" and "Will Mlle. Lenglen beat Mrs. Chambers?" This confidence in Patterson and the French lady Champion was all the more remarkable because, while

Patterson had already suffered defeat this season from three players all of whom were in the lists at Wimbledon, Mlle Lenglen had never played on a grass court till a month ago. Yes the confidence was there and it was not misplaced.

It was quickly settled. From start to finish there was only one man in it. And that one was Patterson. He went for his shot every time, almost contemptuously; and it came off more often than it failed.

A tremendous service, a rush to the net, a neat volley or a devastating smash – that was his plan of campaign. McLoughnir hit over again, in fact. But it served him well. Brookes seemed nerveless, and to care little whether he won or lost. He was not the Brookes of old. Six months in hospital have told their tale.

MAY 17ᵀᴴ, 1941

CURIOSITIES OF BALL-GAMES

BY FRANK W. LANE

INSTANCES ARE NOT uncommon of players or spectators being injured during ball games, but a case occurred in America of a player injuring himself – and in a game of skittles. Tennis players have many self-imposed handicaps. The strangest tennis match I have ever heard of was one played at night in pitch darkness, with phosphorescent balls. The village constable arrived and, throwing the light of his flash-lamp on the scene, demanded to know what was going on. After being satisfied he consented to act as ball-boy.

Cricket has provided several "believe it or not" situations. During a match at Nairobi when the jungle started on the outskirts of the town a hard pull to leg from a batsman had sent the ball almost into the undergrowth. A lion sprang out and began to play with it. What followed is best described in the words of the present Secretary of India Mr. I. S. Amery who records the incident in his book *Days of Fresh Air*:

> "THE BATSMEN WENT ON RUNNING TILL ENOUGH FIELDERS ARRIVED TO CHASE OFF THE LION"

"The fielding side claimed 'lost ball', which the umpire disallowed as contrary to the visible facts of the situation and the batsmen went on running till enough fielders arrived to chase off the lion and retrieve the chewed up remnants of the ball."

A man once placed a 500-page telephone directory four feet in front of a tee and drove off. The ball tore through the directory and rolled another 100 yds. A golf ball has crashed through a door of quarter-inch wood and travelled over 100 yds. on the other side, as is illustrated in the picture.

A golf ball killed a cow near Dover a few years ago. Among other creatures that have been killed in the same way are a fox, hares and partridges. A professional golfer once bagged a brace of water wagtails with one ball. But of all "kills" by golf balls I think that the most amazing was a two pound trout. Presumably the fish jumped just as the ball was flying over a stream and trout and ball collided.

A man in America gets his living by retrieving lost balls. He bought a car, two collapsible boats and a rake. He obtained retrieving rights with big clubs and in ten years he retrieved over 1,000,000 balls.

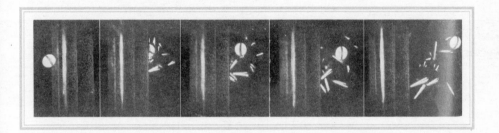

AUGUST 15ᵀᴴ, 1931

THE CROWD AND THE GATE

BY BERNARD DARWIN

I N THE GOLFING books of reference there used to be (perhaps there is still, but I am at the moment too lazy to look for it) an odd item of miscellaneous information. It was to the effect that gate money was first charged at a golf match some time in the 'nineties, when Douglas Rolland and Jack White met in an exhibition match at Chesterford Park, near Cambridge.

We have got tolerably well accustomed to gate money since those days, even though we still have at the backs of our minds a notion that golf, alone among games, is a free spectacle. Nevertheless, gate money on the links of St. Andrews does, at the first hearing, give something of a shock. Obviously it had to come. The Championship Committee did wisely to deliver a friendly ultimatum to the Town Council that there could be no Open Championship at St. Andrews in 1933 unless there was a charge for admission, and the Town Council have done equally wisely

in accepting the situation and applying to Parliament for a Provisional Order to enable them to charge. The Amateur Championship last year was the writing on the wall. Goodness knows it was bad enough as it was for some of the poor wretches who were run over by Mr. Bobby Jones's crowd.

So far as it is humanly possible, that must never happen again, and it is to be hoped that gate money will prevent it. I remember that when gate money was first tried at Muirfield there were many gloomy prognostications. It was said that the great heart of the Scottish people would not stand such a thing and would break riotously in. This prophecy proved quite unfounded; no doubt some persons who have a constitutional objection to paying for anything got in; unobserved, by the sandhills, but it was a negligible number, and there was no thought of rioting.

> "IT WAS SAID THAT THE GREAT HEART OF THE SCOTTISH PEOPLE WOULD NOT STAND SUCH A THING AND WOULD BREAK RIOTOUSLY IN"

I should rather be looking forward hopefully to the experiment. It must succeed, for St. Andrews without a championship will not bear thinking about.

FEBRUARY 7ᵀᴴ, 1925

MODERN BOXING ON EXHIBITION

THE SPORT IS frequently misunderstood and there are still large numbers of people who can find nothing admirable, amusing or even remotely interesting in it, because they regard boxing as a merely ugly bashing of man by man for money; or, at the best, and among amateurs, as the bashing of man by man as an outlet for primitive and detestable energy. The current exhibition at the Sporting Gallery, from whence these pictures came, might go a long way to cure the most hardened objector – if only by the splendid way of laughter.

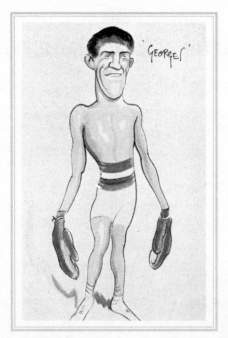

MAY 30TH, 1931

HOW POLO SHOULD BE TAUGHT

BY CAPTAIN C. T. I. ROARK

I HAVE RIDDEN ponies and horses almost ever since I was born, have never been away from them, have played polo for more years than I care to confess, and have watched and thought about the game from every possible angle; my opinion and impressions may possibly be thought of some value.

I do not hesitate to state that, in my opinion, if any beginner really bothers to study and proceeds along the lines mapped out for his guidance, he will "arrive", and be able to strike the ball far better within a shorter space of time than if he commences as most players do, not really understanding what the general plan of the game is, but just armed with a stick and a ball, and more often than not riding a pony entirely unsuitable for the job. Even more emphasis might, I think, be put on the advice to beginners as to getting "suitable" ponies and not "overhorsing" themselves.

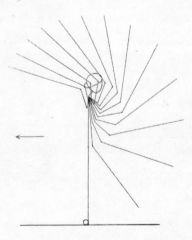

Diagram of the Near-side Forehand Swing.

JANUARY 8TH, 1921

THE ART OF RUGBY FOOTBALL

BY E. H. D. SEWELL

WE ARRIVE NOW at "The Vital Moment." This is the instant in every Rugby football match which tells most on the emotions of the onlooker. It is first cousin to that fraction of a second of time during a big firework display which produces the "Ah!" of assembled thousands as the rocket bursts in the darkness. This is the moment for which coaches coach which, in a sense, serves to stifle genuine forward play by training front-rankers (of the team, not of the scrum) to become rather too much of a co-operative society for the quick and true delivery of the ball to the back division. It is certainly the vital moment in the game, which is more often won and lost on the merits or demerits of this forwards-made pass from the scrum than on those of any other "incident" of the play.

JUNE 20TH, 1925

THE MORE COMPLEAT CRICKETER

FIELDING

O F ALL DEPARTMENTS of the game, fielding is the most important, hence I give it pride of place. No cricketer, be he ever so great a batsman or supreme a bowler, is worthy of his place in his side if he be a slovenly and careless fieldsman. If you are quick, accurate and alert in the field, you go in to bat with at least thirty runs to your credit before a single run has been scored actually from your bat. Reversely, a slipshod attitude in the field merely betokens that you, as a batsman, will have to score thirty runs before you can truly be said to have added a single run to the credit of your side.

A bad fieldsman, who has obviously taken no trouble to improve himself, is the sure sign of a bad cricketer, bad not only in actual execution, but, what is of more importance, bad in spirit – a man who will have an injurious effect upon the general morale of the rest of his team, as, inversely, a fine fieldsman will exercise a most fine and encouraging one.

Fielding must not be looked on as "a soft job" and a time when you can take a peaceful rest from the "greater" and more "strenuous calls" that batting and bowling make upon you. The golden rule, therefore, is to display the utmost concentration – which is the logical outcome of interest – upon every single ball bowled throughout the innings; the senses, faculties and nerves being keyed up to the highest pitch of expectancy.

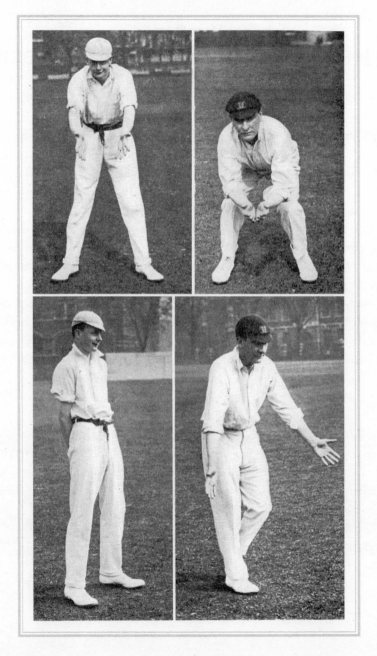

APRIL 6ᵀᴴ, 1912

THE UNIVERSITY BOAT RACE

An exciting description of a University Boat Race in which there was no winner. On the following Monday the rival crews met once more, Oxford prevailing by three lengths.

OR THE SAKE of future readers it is desirable that the extraordinary occurrences of Saturday should be accurately set down and described. The annals of boat-racing do not contain the record of anything similar. Both the University boats filled. The Boat Race instituted in 1829 and since then there has only been one occasion on which a crew sank. This occurred in 1859. On Saturday nobody expected anything so extraordinary to occur. The water, it is true, was rough; but it was not so bad as in 1898, when the Cambridge boat shipped water at the very beginning of the course. The river was certainly uninviting. At 11.43 the boats started on water that was as unfit and disagreeable as it well could be.

They reached the Mile Post in 5 mins. 18 sec. which has the distinction of being the longest time for that distance in the history of the race. Both boats, as a matter of fact, had been taking in considerable quantities of water, which spouted from the riggers and came tumbling in about the feet of the oarsmen. Cambridge had suffered most from this cause, and as her gunwale lowered, the water poured in more and more, till at Harrods' Wharf the cox had to turn the boat to the shore, as it was evident that she was going to sink altogether. This she did, the stern going down first. The men jumped out, as at the place where they were it was impossible to empty and right the boat and proceed. So far Oxford had had the better of the luck; but at the centre arch of Hammersmith Bridge very rough water awaited them. They struggled past the Doves; but the boat sank at last at Chiswick Steps. Mr. Bourne slipped over the side, the other men followed his example, and they began to drag the boat ashore in what must have been bitterly cold water until they were immersed to the armpits.

COUNTRY LIFE

MOTOR SHOW NUMBER

On Sale Friday
OCTOBER 24, 1952

TWO SHILLINGS

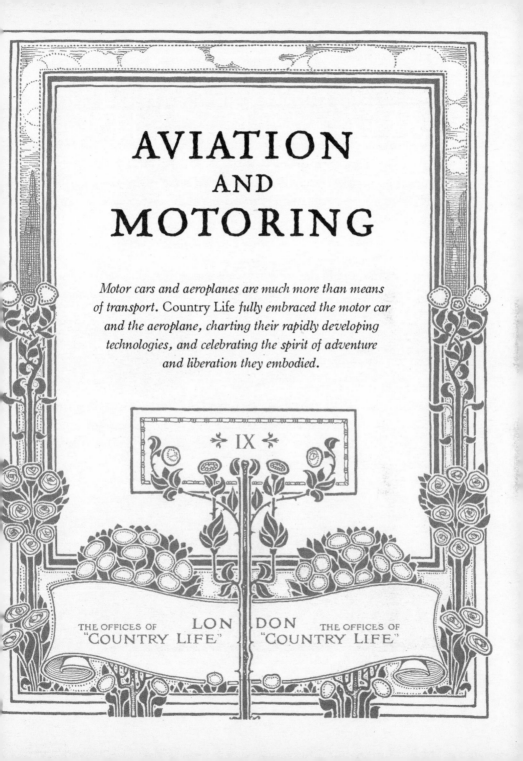

AVIATION
AND
MOTORING

Motor cars and aeroplanes are much more than means of transport. Country Life *fully embraced the motor car and the aeroplane, charting their rapidly developing technologies, and celebrating the spirit of adventure and liberation they embodied.*

❖ IX ❖

THE OFFICES OF   LONDON   THE OFFICES OF
"COUNTRY LIFE"   "COUNTRY LIFE"

NEW CARS TESTED

I N JUNE LAST year I described my first test of the then new Alvis Speed Twenty. I then came to the conclusion that this car was capable of holding its own with anything in the world at anywhere near its price in the fast touring car class, and a renewed test of the 1934 vehicle has only confirmed my opinion.

PERFORMANCE

The maximum speed of the car was a good honest 85 m.p.h. I attained 80 m.p.h. from a standing start in exactly 32 secs. The top gear performance was really good for an engine of such moderate dimensions, and very little use had to be made of the ignition lever to prevent pinking on Benzole mixture.

THE ROAD HOLDING

This is a point which interested me particularly in this car. It was the first time that I have had a really fast car out with independent front wheel springing and steering. At speed the behaviour of the front could

only be described as magnificent. The car would glide along near its maximum with one's finger resting on the rim of the wheel and not a trace of a shock coming back through the steering. On potholes at high or low speed there was no suggestion of discomfort, and one never had to wrestle with the steering.

GENERAL POINTS OF DESIGN

Three S.U. carburettors arc used, and the mixture distribution seems to be as nearly perfect as possible, as the pick-up of the engine is instantaneous. The engine design is neat, and everything is easily accessible, while special care has been taken in the design of the water spaces so as to keep vital points cool. The overhead valves are actuated by push rods and special dual ignition is used, consisting of a polar inductor magneto adapted by use of special switches and a high-tension coil to act as coil ignition for starting or in the unlikely event of magneto failure.

COACHWORK

The Vanden Plas open touring body has extremely good lines and is also very comfortable. This firm has a unique experience in building open touring bodies for fast cars, and I can speak from experience, having owned one of their bodies on a Bentley for five years. Incidentally, the back seats are very much more comfortable than is usual with this type of bodywork, and the all-weather equipment is very complete and serviceable.

APRIL 21ST, 1934

"DRIVING LICENCE AND LICENCES"

It was, in fact, in 1934 that a competency test was first introduced.

TO THE EDITOR OF "COUNTRY LIFE."

SIR,—I cordially agree with the proposal in your last week's Country Note under this title. May I suggest that the following would carry out your proposal in a practical form. It would exactly fit in to the "neat little cloth-bound book" on the page opposite the licence itself, where it would be a constant reminder to the driver of his obligations.—E. H.

IN taking out this licence I acknowledge that neglect by me of any of the following points in road usage is a grave fault and likely to be the cause of accidents.

" CUTTING IN "

KEEPING TO THE CROWN OF THE ROAD SO AS TO PREVENT OTHERS PASSING

IGNORING OR FAILING TO GIVE PROPER SIGNALS

PASSING ON BENDS OR BLIND BRIDGES

EMERGING FROM BYROADS OR GATEWAYS WITHOUT CAUTION

PARKING ON BENDS

I understand that in the event of an accident resulting from my failure to observe any of these points, or in the event of my failing to stop after an accident, I am liable to have this licence withdrawn.

Signed . . . .

SEPTEMBER 8ᵀᴴ, 1928

DANGEROUS DOINGS

I AM AWARE THAT in these days the majority of occupations – from coal-mining to crossing the road – are dangerous, but in those other occupations necessity is at the back of our acceptance of the risk – or it seems to us that it is. We cross the road because, like a hen, we believe it to be necessary to get to the other side.

But whatever method civilisation chooses to adopt for killing us – and whether the process be long or short – we can have, individually, but little to say in the matter in the daily business of getting our living. In our sport or recreation the position is quite different. That is why, when being driven in a motor car, we resent it so fiercely when we are being driven too fast. We are not afraid to die, but when we are out to enjoy ourselves we do not intend that some other individual shall arbitrarily decide the manner in ·which we shall meet death.

> "I WAS WEARING ONE YELLOW SOCK AND ONE GREEN ONE"

Sometimes, of course, there are additional or peculiar reasons for the resentment we feel against the fast drivers. I have myself twice had occasion (necessity compelling) to change my clothes completely when being driven in a taxi-cab too fast across London. Each time my fury was a mute fury, because any resort to bellowings and window-tappings would necessarily have drawn the driver's attention to my half-nakedness. He would then have refuse to drive me any farther at all. But my fury was the greater from the realisation that at the inquest, after the crash, it would come out that at the moment of impact I was wearing one yellow sock and one green one. All sorts of things might then have come out. The driver, who would be sure, himself, to be thrown clear would also be sure to remember that "he thought I looked queer" when I hailed him. Well, of course I look queer but I do not want the thing to be placarded all over London.

WOOD IS PETROL IN WARTIME: METHODS OF GENERATING GAS FROM WOOD AND CHARCOAL

THE PROBLEM OF supplies of petrol in wartime is not one which can be ignored. There will be little available for private use, and the country house-owner who is dependent for water and light and transport on oil may well wonder what is likely to happen if war comes. It is for this reason that Continental experiments with wood in place of oil are so interesting. In England we utilise remarkably little wood except in the smoky open fireplaces of Tudor farms. In France, on the other hand, the somewhat unreliable central-heating systems of country *chateaux* are run on wood. If you penetrate the basement you will probably find an affair like a small gasworks and be told it is the *chauffage central*. The country gentleman in France has woodlands, and

his coppice wood is used in this way. The long fire-boxes of the furnaces – there may be a range of six or more – take relatively long wood, and it at least works.

From this thrifty use of cordwood it was not a long step to consider whether wood could be used to generate gas on which a motor car or lorry or an electric light installation could be run. Work has now more than passed the experimental stage, and lorries can be quite successfully run on wood. It is not so good as petrol, and it is dearer and more trouble, but it is quite practical.

We are a coal-producing country, and coal is available except in emergency. Coal in sparing quantities would be available – with no ready means of turning it into mobile power. In the last war coal-gas was used for cars by means of balloon-like gas containers fixed to their roofs and needing frequent recharging at the gas works. But wood is at the door. It would be a dirty, smoky business loading up the old truck or running the "Lister," but it would keep things going, even if industrial nerve-centres got dislocated.—H. B. C. P.

"THE THIN END OF THE WEDGE"

To the Editor of "Country Life."

Sir,—To anyone without prejudice it must be clear that excessive speed of vehicles is one of the commonest causes of road accidents (if not the chief cause); further, it is the one factor, or should be, which is under the direct control of drivers.

Whatever may be the contributing causes of an accident, it is obvious that the higher the speed of a vehicle the less time to avoid the errors of others, or to deal with any unforeseen circumstances which may arise. I feel I must apologise for stating at such length the obvious facts, but they cannot, I am sure, be denied. It is of course, equally clear that high speed in itself is not necessarily dangerous, and that while a speed of 50 m.p.h may often be quite safe, one of 10 m.p.h. may be, in certain circumstances, highly dangerous.

Statistics showed that most of the street accidents in London occurred at speeds of less than 10 m.p.h. But these figures are of little, if any, value, since there is no means of determining the speed of cars at the time of an accident. Even if the figures are correct, they prove nothing, for most drivers in danger of accident would pull up, and cars can reduce speed very quickly. A quite fair conclusion to draw from this 10 miles per hour figure is that it proves that the drivers in question were going just that amount too fast, and were, therefore, unable to pull up or slow down in time to avoid collision.

It is scarcely surprising that some public interest should be roused, for a daily road death toll of sixteen for Great Britain can hardly be regarded as a satisfactory state of affairs. The extraordinary thing is that this high rate of mortality is so little noticed; if it were to occur, say, on the railways, the papers would be full of scare headings, but, as it is, the deaths from road accidents produce very little comment.

As has been recently pointed out, it is with the coroner's juries that the responsibility lies for dealing adequately with these cases, the existing laws being adequate if enforced. A considerable degree of responsibility must also rest on those who so frequently proclaim, with an appearance of authority, that high road speeds are not dangerous, and that speed has nothing to do with accidents.—R. J. CLAUSEN

MARCH 28TH, 1925

A POSTCARD ADVENTURE

To the Editor of "Country Life."

SIR, —We were having dinner in a small restaurant in Grenoble when in walked a young fellow in full motorcycling regalia. He made a rapid tour of the tables and, without saying a word, placed at the side of each diner a postcard bearing his photograph and a brief announcement that he was making a tour of the world by motorcycle, all expenses being covered by the sale of these cards. Having finished his tour of the tables he re-began it immediately to collect the cards he had distributed, and as far as I could tell he obtained from about four diners as many francs. Afterwards I had a chat with him, but, as the evening was his best time for selling cards, he asked to be excused, and so we made an appointment for 8 a.m. the next morning so that I might get a photograph of him and his travelling companion – who, at this time, was outside the restaurant in the biting cold guarding the machine. This latter turned out to be a Gillette two-stroke of 350 c.c., with all-chain transmission and two-speed gear and clutch, the two men taking turns at driving and sitting on the pillion seat. They had left Brussels on December 18th, 1924, and, having covered Holland, were

> "SO RELUCTANT WERE THE STOLID DUTCH TO SHOW PRACTICAL APPRECIATION OF THIS SPORTING ENTERPRISE"

now on their way to Riviera sunshine, whence they were bound for Spain, North Africa, Palestine, Turkey, Russia, Germany, Denmark, Norway, England and America. Constant Leon Bisman, who can speak five languages, though his companion, Albert Pole, seemed to be limited to French, told us that in Holland they had had to be content with nothing but bread and cheese for food, so reluctant were the stolid Dutch to show practical appreciation of this sporting enterprise, even if they felt any, which is doubtful. In France the travellers had been more successful, but I could not help wondering how they would fare in Turkey and Russia, and even in parts of England. Apparently, Scotland was not included in their itinerary. As the photograph shows, our morning appointment found the adventurers with a flat tyre, but this must not be taken as an indication that the machine was in the precise condition in which it was intended to be for the whole journey. But, apart from this tyre, it was so. There were no more luggage and no more spares than those accommodated in the limited toolbags of the motorcycle!—J.

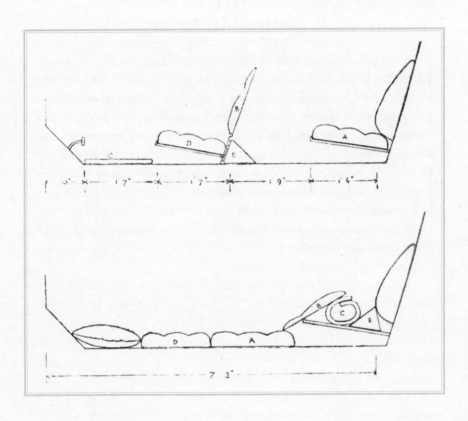

APRIL 29TH, 1922

"OCCASIONAL CAMPING BY MOTOR CAR"

To the Editor of "Country Life."

Sir,—Mr. Meyrick Jones' article in your issue of April 1st with this attractive title has doubtless opened the eyes of many of your readers to the fact that, subject to a little contrivance, they have in their car a new and fascinating possession – a travelling sleeping apartment. This possession opens out a new pleasure to anyone addicted to sleeping out in the summer months, and for those who prefer a shelter over their heads the hood and side-curtains provide one ready to hand. The ideal to be sought for is a wood off the road, but provided with a drivable track, and close to a stream. I stipulate for a stream as no camping place is worthy that does not provide a morning swim, or at least sufficient running water for the morning toilet.

My own experiences have been in a modest way with a small touring four-seater namely the 11.9 h.p. "Standard," which owing to its easily detachable front seats and admirable hood, is particularly well adapted for converting into a bed. The diagrams will explain themselves, showing how the car can be converted into quite a comfortable bed for two people who can, for a night or two, put up with rather limited accommodation.

The addition of one or two air cushions to act as pillows at the head and another to form an extension at the foot – or a rolled up coat does as well – and in five minutes the bed is contrived.—Ambrose Heal

THE AUTOMOBILE WORLD.

By The Hon. MAYNARD GREVILLE.

HITCH AND HIKE

FOR THOSE OF a roving disposition there are few things more satisfying than the United States' entertainment of hitch and hike. Clean collars are the first essential of the successful exponent of hitch and hike. It is little short of marvellous what a clean collar will do to retrieve the reputation of one whose trousers are becoming perceptibly thin at the seat and knee. The element of chance enters into the game, and many a born gambler has, no doubt, released a life-long repression on the road. After seating oneself next the driver a tactful query soon elicits the information as to the distance one is likely to traverse at his side. Sometimes one is informed with awful gravity that one's *pro tem.* chauffeur is turning off the road in half a mile, in which case one does not inform him that one's destination lies half a continent farther on. Whatever the answer, one expresses surprise and delight, and then if one's companion is talkative, one draws him out.

> "CLEAN COLLARS ARE THE FIRST ESSENTIAL OF THE SUCCESSFUL EXPONENT OF HITCH AND HIKE"

To average 150 miles a day is fair, but there are those with very white collars who manage to do as much as 200. "Take no thought for the morrow" is the motto of the auto hobo, and one can never guess an hour ahead where one is likely to "hit the hay".

Discarded railway sleepers are invaluable at night, and many a desert landscape is illuminated by the fires of these 6 ft. logs. So, after all, the joys of hitch and hike can hardly be exaggerated, and whether it is better to grow old seeking the means to pay for the petrol to carry one across the continent or feed the fires of youth with the glories of Nature and liberty is open to question, but the adventurous youth of America can rarely resist the temptation of at least one spell of what Masefield describes so aptly:

Only the road and the dawn, the
Sun, the wind and the rain,
And the watch fire under the stars,
And sleep and the road again.

—X. Y. Z.

"LIKE A DOG, ONE SHAKES ON ARISING."

JULY 6TH, 1918

LIGHTER THAN AIR

BY WARD MUIR

UPON AN OTHERWISE empty tableland some few miles from the coast, stand two cathedrals side by side. In the dusk of the evening and in the midst of a barren but beautiful countryside whose peace was a delicious contrast to London's turmoil there was something uncanny about those stark outlines silhouetted by the sunset. To what strange god had such temples been erected, so far from any city? Lo, the answer to that question was manifest at once. For, aloft against the flaming heaven, a queer shape moved – an oblong bubble with a little black parallelogram suspended beneath its belly – pushing itself through the air, down and across the sky in the direction of the nearer cathedral. And pigmies ran forth on to the tableland at a bugle's summons; scores of tiny blue-clad figures preparing to capture the bubble and, with ropes, tow it in through the vast doorway's arch to the sheltering safety of its shrine.

What will Man do next? one asks oneself, partly in awe and partly with a hysterical sense of the absurd, when first confronted by an airship. What will be the next glorious myth or hateful nightmare that this ever-restless biped will insist on realising? What ridiculous lie will he make to come true? What sweet and unsophisticated landscape will he next trespass upon with some mad manifestation of the marvels of science and engineering? Here was a spot so remote from what we call civilisation that its few scattered farms and hamlets bore every sign of age; the lane along which my motor car had whirled me was deep-cut with centuries of slow farm-cart traffic and plodding hobnailed boots; near us upon the shore were ancient fishing villages pursuing an ancient fishing trade.

It was intimated to me that as soon as a sea mist, which hemmed in the cathedral's open door like a curtain of cotton-wool, had lifted, I might accompany the crew of one of the Coastals upon a flight. For now the mist was breaking; a bugle blew; the hands were unfastening the ropes, the first ship began to slide from the cathedral's gloom into the sunshine; and I was told that the time had come for me to don my leather overcoat, my flier cap and goggles and climb aboard.

JULY 5TH, 1930

SOARING FLIGHT

WHEN GLIDING WAS first described as a coming sport in COUNTRY LIFE, many people were sceptical, but the sanguine prophecies then made have been more than fulfilled. Herr Kronfeld has been giving, near Lewes, some demonstrations of soaring flight which have aroused the wonder and admiration of all who saw them. He has ascended in his sailplane, the Wein, and has flown with the completest assurance sometimes for hours on end. His flights have provided beautiful spectacles and have also given testimony to his skill and to the advances that have been made in this branch of aviation. His monoplane has the appearance of a bird, with wide, narrow wings and carefully streamlined fuselage. Seated in the Wein, Herr Kronfeld is flicked into the air from the brow of a slope by the usual system. A double length of elastic shock absorber is passed through a hook under his aeroplane and the two ends are held by two parties of five assistants each. The two parties move forward until the elastic is taut, and then Herr Kronfeld gives the command "release." Those who have been holding his machine back let go, and it leaps into the air with the motion of a diver from a spring board and then poises itself in the air-stream which is deflected upwards by the rising ground. Without a sound the sailplane flies and gradually it turns with scarcely any " bank." As it turns down-wind it loses height. It makes a complete circuit and comes up again into wind, now climbing strongly. After attaining height, Herr Kronfeld may fly along the crest of the slope, climbing at times, and at times losing height. In this way he may travel for anything up to seventy or a hundred miles.

"THE SENSATIONS OF FLIGHT UNSPOILT BY THE NOISE AND VIBRATION OF AN ENGINE"

The principle of sail-planing consists in the use of wind currents which have been deflected upwards as a result of the formation of the ground, or of radiation or of the upward currents found associated with *cumulus* and *cumulo-nimbus* clouds.

The sport of gliding, as I mentioned in COUNTRY LIFE last February, has achieved great popularity in Germany and America. It provides people with a means of tasting the sensations of flight unspoilt by the noise and vibration of an engine. The recent demonstrations have instilled into many Englishmen the desire to soar, and, with the aid of the numerous clubs already formed, they will soon be able to fulfil their wish.—OLIVER STEWART

APRIL 5ᵀᴴ, 1930

AIR YACHTING

BY OLIVER STEWART

O NE OF THE most interesting of the specialised types of aircraft now in process of evolution is the air yacht. It is a recent conception and is even yet in the earliest stages of development. But it possesses certain features which make so strong an appeal to the imagination and which seem so attractive to those who have an affection for the sea, that it is probable that in time it may attain a popularity comparable with that of larger kinds of surface yacht. It extends the scope of its owner in a way that no other craft can do; it offers him a pleasurable kind of motion, and at the same time it brings within his reach places which are too far away to be visited by steam or sail with a short holiday period. On these accounts at least it is certain to attain a measure of popularity as a pleasure vehicle.

The air yacht is a type of craft which owes its conception mainly to designers and manufacturers in this country. And it is only just that this should be so, seeing that it is in the direct line of descent from the surface yacht, which owes its development largely to British builders. It shows a vitality which suggests that it will eventually find favour among those who take their pleasures on the sea. The time may yet come, though it is probably still a long way away, when, in Cowes Road, the white wings of aircraft will be seen among those other white wings which must always remain the aristocrats of the yachting world.

HON. ROBIN COCHRANE, SON OF LADY DUNDONALD.

SCHOOLDAYS

"Making good use of gas masks and bad use of air
rifles should be a part of every schoolboy's education..."
Country Life *covered every important milestone in a*
young man's life.

✦ X ✦

THE OFFICES OF   LON   DON   THE OFFICES OF
"COUNTRY LIFE"   "COUNTRY LIFE"

JULY 18ᵀᴴ, 1923

BOYS ON PONIES

A MAN ONCE gave in nine words a reason for killing himself that was more adequate than most men could give for being allowed to live. "I am tired," he wrote, with a fine simplicity, "of all the buttoning and unbuttoning." The coroner said it was temporary insanity, but the unofficial view was that the man was temporarily sane. All small boys would agree with the latter verdict, and it is therefore prudent, when teaching boys to ride, not to lay too much stress on the importance of a boy being able to strip his own saddle, or his own bridle and carry out the thousand and one buttoning and unbuttoning processes which are, naturally, so interesting to the horse-master and, rightly, so boring to a boy. The man who cannot realise this may or may not be fitted to command a cavalry regiment – he is totally unfit to teach a boy to ride. And if you want your boy to be taught to ride you had better sound the proposed teacher as to the rest of his views on the subject.

Horsemanship and democracy have this in common, that an equal amount of cant and hypocrisy is talked by the devotees of both. To bore a boy with riding school and the "minor ailments" and expect him to become a keen young horseman is nearly as futile as to preach the federation of man to a Russian peasant. The boy and the Bolshevik will go round the corner together – looking for something to smash.

"First take your boy" – you can almost do the thing on the principle of a cooking recipe, or, preferably someone else's boy. In the latter case you will neither be so annoyed when he shows himself to be frightened, stupid and forgetful, nor will you be so extravagantly proud when he proves himself to be courageous, quick-witted and apt to learn. Being a normal boy, he will inevitably be all these in turn but on your intelligent, as well as sympathetic, reading of the outstanding traits in his character depends your whole chance of success.

The excruciating period of the first lessons will only end when the boy himself refuses any longer to hold on by the teacher's neck, and asks to be allowed to ride alone. This, if you are the teacher, heralds the dawn of a new day for you. You must not allow the exhilaration of the prospect of escaping death by strangulation to dim your judgement. It will start with the request that "We won't have the leading-rein to-day." You will reject that request and the next one two minutes later. Your charge is now loose. For better or worse, for poorer and not richer, he has joined the ranks of the Horsemen – those intolerant men who, while thinking it wrong to criticise the honesty of a friend or his faithfulness to his wife, will persistently insult and decry his horsemanship – which the majority of them secretly think to be a virtue infinitely more important than either of the others.

SCOUTS IN THE WOODS

To the Editor of "Country Life."

Sir,—Some months ago when taking a spell at the burning of some trimmings from a plantation I happened to remark to my host that here, indeed, was work that would be congenial to Scouts. Apparently he took immediate action, for some weeks later I was asked to time a further visit for when the camp would be in being. Some twenty boys were there, happily located on a gentle incline. With river, punts and bathing station in proximity. Thus, for a start there was bathing and boating, added to which was my own contribution by the way of a B.S.A. air rifle together with unlimited rounds of ammunition. Some of the boys had brought fishing rods, others rabbit snares, so the sporting amenities of the trip were well covered. Add to these a day with the otter hounds, and the cup of joy was full.

> "ADD TO THESE A DAY WITH THE OTTER HOUNDS, AND THE CUP OF JOY WAS FULL"

Some definite programme of work is desirable for boys, even on a holiday, but care must be taken to avoid exploiting them in the interests of cheap labour. Donations in the way of vegetables and food, not to forget a very large cake and substantial money prizes for forestry, easily disposed of this difficulty.

These and other interesting facts were appreciatively received, and well the moral was applied, for at the end of the fortnight a strip of covert some 200 yds. long by 60 yds. wide had been pruned and cleared so as to require no more further attention for a dozen years or more.—M. B.

AUGUST 20TH, 1921

FACTORY AND PUBLIC SCHOOL BOYS

W E LEARN THAT the experiment at New Romney was in every way a great success. Our readers will remember that the party was composed of boys from the Public Schools and boys of the working classes. Originally it was stated that the conception and carrying out of the enterprise were due to the Duke of York supporting the project with his influence and also with his spirited endeavour to see that the young people should, in his own words, "have a jolly good time." Further, our information is that he intends that this experiment shall be repeated annually for five years. Everybody who recognises the fault of our educational system, that it does not do enough to make good citizens as well as scholars, will rejoice at the announcement.

> "THE FAULT OF OUR EDUCATIONAL SYSTEM, THAT IT DOES NOT DO ENOUGH TO MAKE GOOD CITIZENS AS WELL AS SCHOLARS"

There is no country in the world where the division of classes is so rigid as it is with us. Perhaps we should have said, as it is with England. In democratic Scotland there is much less of that kind of distinction, and, no doubt, there is an inheritance from the old parish schools. If there is any fault to be found with the Public School boy it is that he is only too well organised. He is too frequently engaged in doing what everybody else is doing at the same time, and this is a great obstacle to the development of individuality and initiative. Of course, one would not say that all reach the same standard and that some do not fall very far below it, but on the whole the university students are admirable, yet when they come to take their places as captains of industry the defect is discovered that they do not really know much about the labouring men whom they employ.

The boys were in the wildest high spirits from the first day to the last. When anyone made a speech they punctuated it with loud cheers. When they were left to themselves the echoes rang with their laughter and conversation, and the discovery was made that after all there is not such a great difference between boys of different classes, the separation is really artificial. Even in regard to manners, one who is a very good judge said that there was but little to choose between them. It was one of the happy thoughts of the Duke of York to take them to New Romney because of its aerodrome and the hutments put up for the staff, which could be utilised for lodging the boys. Each boy from a Public School had to chum with a boy from a factory, and they seemed to get on very well together.

APRIL 30TH, 1910

THE SAVAGE AND THE AIR-GUN

HE SAVAGE WAS home for his summer holidays. He was ten years of age, and, despite his white skin and English blood, he was still at heart a simple barbarian. He had the good qualities of the natural savage – his courage, his generosity and his simplicity – and, in addition, he had his faults. It is possible that these last may reveal themselves in this, to a humanitarian, slightly painful tale.

Well, as the Savage remarked to me in telling the story, no man could have spoken more fairly. He thanked his uncle for the present, as a grateful nephew should, and next morning as ever was he went out with studied secrecy and bought that air-gun. He had had his eye upon the piece for quite a while, but it had always been rather beyond his means. During the holidays his father seemed to believe in fairly frequent doles rather than lump sums. The Savage, for his part, did not believe in this method. He conceived that it rather destroyed a fellow's self-respect to have to be always asking.

So the Savage slipped a few slugs into the pocket of his breeches, did a little scouting to see that the coast was clear, and got into the open air without trouble from any foolish grown-up people. He reached the shrubbery by one of the side paths and crept upon his stomach to the fringe of the trees to see if a moose or anything of that sort was grazing upon the croquet lawn...

TALES
OF
COUNTRY
LIFE.

THE SAVAGE AND
THE AIR-GUN.
BY
JOHN BARNETT.

JUNE 25ᵀᴴ, 1943

WHAT EVERY
SCHOOLBOY KNOWS

S IR D'ARCY THOMPSON wrote a letter to *The Times* the other day complaining of the ignorance of young zoologists and the sting of his lash must have fallen on the backs of those who are not zoologists and not young. In an examination for entrance scholarships he had asked in what parts of the world there could be found a number of "common animals" and set out with some little contempt the answer received. At first glance we, who are not being examined, can see one or two answers which might be vulgarly described as "sitters". We do know that it is a confusion of thought and spelling to say that "llamas" come from Tibet, because we were brought up with the poem which ends

> I would eat a missionary,
> Hat and coat and hymn book too.

But when we come to *ornithorhyncus* our learning rapidly decreases and there are others over which we feel far from confident. "Every schoolboy knows," said Macaulay; "who imprisoned Montezuma, and who strangled Atahualpa," and many people are painfully conscious that they did not know even when they were schoolboys. More than ever does it become one of the consolations of growing older that we shall never again have to enter for an examination.

JULY 25TH, 1908

SCHOOL CADET CORPS

"To the outside world a school cadet corps implies a few parades in every term and the annual appearance of a shooting eight at Bisley. Class-firing, too, is none too easy to organise; each cadet should fire his course of fifty shots on Service or miniature range, according to his size, and, taking the average number of cadets in a school to be 100, some 5,000 cartridges must be discharged in a season in the most careful supervision. Bearing in mind that many establishments have to visit ranges miles away from them, that the claims of cricket, not to mention work, must be considered, and that the weather only admits of a very brief season for the rifle shooting, it will be allowed that the authorities have something to grapple with; and grapple with it

they do most successfully. But, after all, shooting is to a corps its very life-blood, and though the task may be Herculean, it has somehow to be accomplished if the institution is to exist at all.

Other portions there are of military training which might be allowed to slide, but which the boys make their own as surely as they do the rifle. First of these is signalling, and in many schools will be found those who have mastered not only the semaphore and the Morse but the heliograph. The first of these is easy, and may be learnt in a term, but the two latter demand months of painstaking practice before messages can be speedily read and transmitted. It would hardly be thought that the drudgery connected with entrenchments would appeal to boys, but I am informed that at Eastbourne, at any rate, where this form of exercise has been instituted, volunteers for the spade and pick are by no means loath to come forward.

Not the least important parts of the cadets' work is done each year in camp at Aldershot, and one of the greatest pleasures in the life of a commanding officer is to see the readiness with which so many give up a week of their holidays. No less gratifying to witness is the splendid way in which they perform their arduous labours when they have exchanged the dormitory for the tent.

GAS-MASKS AND CATAPULTS

D R. WATTS'S WELL-KNOWN views on mischief for idle hands have lately been illustrated in a letter from the secretary of the Royal Society for the Prevention of Cruelty to Animals. It appears that naughty and ingenious little boys have discovered in gas-masks a rich mine of rubber suitable for catapults, and that birds, cats and dogs are suffering accordingly. Of course they ought not to do it, but it is hard to be very angry with them, for a catapult is a dreadfully fascinating weapon, the more so as it is nearly always short-lived; it is sooner or later confiscated by some unsympathetic schoolmaster. Yet the complaint does make us reflect that it is almost time we were told what to do with our now mercifully unwanted gas-masks. If the rubber in them is valuable for such purposes as braces, of which there is said to be a shortage, then surely the nation is still salvage-minded and we ought to be told to hand them in.

"FOR A CATAPULT IS A DREADFULLY FASCINATING WEAPON"

DECEMBER 15TH, 1900

THREE EMBRYO SPORTSMEN

To the Editor of "Country Life."

Sir,—My father having been a subscriber to your valuable paper for some years, and seeing some very interesting photographs, I send you a photograph of us, and wish you would be so kind as to put it in your paper. Me and my brothers are ten, eleven, and thirteen years of age, and ride gallops, sometimes too fast for papa. He says that we must ride in Sloan style, but we like the English style best. My father is private trainer for Count Henckel von Donnersmark, and has been out here this last twenty years, It would give him and us much pleasure to see us in your paper.—Fred, Charley and Alfred Vivian, Carlburg, Hungaria.

CURIOSITIES
AND
ODDITIES

Tattoos, a surfeit of smoking and strange bedfellows –
Country Life's pages have always included the
more eccentric indulgences of life.

✦ XI ✦

THE OFFICES OF   LON DON   THE OFFICES OF
"COUNTRY LIFE" | "COUNTRY LIFE"

FEBRUARY 13TH, 1937

FITNESS FOR ALL WHO WILL

BY LORD BADEN-POWELL

Lord Baden-Powell, who started the Scout movement, clearly believed in the importance of exercise for the nation.

THERE IS A big move on – at last – to improve the physique of the nation. I don't know what has drawn our attention to our shortcomings in that direction. Possibly it has been the failure of our athletes to make good showing at the Olympic Games, or the fact that on the average two out of three candidates for the Army are being rejected as unfit, or that (I forget how many) millions of hours of work were lost per annum in the industrial world through ill-health, or the sight of other nations, like Germany and Italy, drilling their rising generation into healthy, hefty manhood.

"OUR GYMNASIA ARE SUPPLIED BY NATURE IN THE SHAPE OF TREES, ROCKS AND MOUNTAINS"

Do we not rather want a good average standard of healthiness and stamina throughout the nation? If so, we are not going to get it through mere physical drill – although that can be very useful as an addition to the training. The problem of physical fitness goes deeper than that, affecting the individual's upbringing and way of life, and thus touching many departments of administration.

In the Boy Scouts we cannot afford gymnasia or paid instructors; our gymnasia are supplied by nature in the shape of trees, rocks and mountains, in God's open air. In cities where such gifts of nature are out of reach, Scouts build themselves very useful apparatus with spars and lashings, and learn climbing on ropes. But independently of these they gain physical development and health through outdoor games, exercises, and activities devised to this end, and which appeal to their liking for sport and adventure, such as boating, swimming, football, biking, camping, etc.

But we are apt to forget in promoting such steps in physical development that we are only trying to apply remedies to defects which exist in our population and which ought not to exist. Take, for instance, the all too common ailment of distorted backbones.

At this time of grave unrest and international jealousies and mutual suspicion, Great Britain has shown a grand example of steady self-discipline, both in her domestic crisis as well as in international affairs. But dangerous times lie ahead, and it is up to every one of us to do his or her bit, however small, towards maintaining that calm outlook and more especially towards instilling into the oncoming generation the same character of mind coupled with better health of body.

HOME-MADE CAMP GYMNASIUM

PARLOUR GAMES

Playing parlour games with a family that is not your own can be a risky business.

THE B.B.C. HAVE evidently hit the public fancy with their spelling bees, and have shown a masterly self-restraint in keeping the standard of spelling required rather low. "There are expressions, you see, Master Copperfield," remarked Uriah Heep, " – Latin words and terms – Mr. Tidd, that are trying to a reader of my 'umble attainments"; and if the words that are chosen were of too trying character, the great spelling heart of the people would cease to beat with so passionate interest. As it is, we all have the chance of exclaiming periodically: "Well, I could have done as well as that" which is extremely soothing. All that is now wanted to make our joy perfect is to hear a schoolmistress make a mistake – a malicious satisfaction hitherto denied us by those resolute and confident ladies. I have been wondering whether an extension of this new form of entertainment is possible so that some of those parlour games in which we have all indulged could be played at the microphone.

"I WAS ALWAYS RATHER GOOD AT CRICKETERS AND MURDERERS"

In all those games which demand the compiling of lists in some small numbers of minutes there is a hideous sensation at once of utter impotence and of the ruthless flight of time. The mind seems to be paralysed, so that when we are asked to write down all the famous people whose name begins with S, we may possibly think of Shakespeare, but never of the rich vein of Smiths. Incidentally, that is one of the games that always seem to need an umpire. It may be only that I am of a quarrelsome and argumentative disposition, and that I used habitually to play this game with a family whose minds moved in altogether different grooves from mine. I was always rather good at cricketers and murderers while they would produce masses of unknown musicians. I positively hated their musicians, and they were very suspicious and disagreeable about my murderers – some of them, I admit, rather obscure ones – so that "the argument ended only with the visit." Still, it is a good game, especially when all those names contained in more than one list are cancelled. This makes highly profitable excursions into the recondite, and, let us say, Selby of Notts (I hope no one will deny that he was a famous cricketer) can be worth more than Shakespeare and Socrates and Solomon put together.

OCTOBER 1ST, 1898

A DEPRAVED HORSE

To the Editor of "Country Life."

SIR,—Can you suggest a remedy for a horse which will not pass a roadside public house? He takes little or no notice of a public house in a town, but almost invariably insists at stopping at every one he comes to along a country road. I suppose that he scents the beer. Nothing will induce him to stir till his rider has been served, or till he considers, as I can only suppose, a proper period of time has elapsed to admit of his being served, and then he goes off gaily enough, to repeat the performance further on. He is a good hack in other respects, and was bought from a dealer who professes to know nothing of his antecedents. It is quite clear that he had a bibulous master at one time. If you could give me any advice I should be extremely grateful.—EQUESTRIAN

> "I SUPPOSE THAT HE SCENTS THE BEER"

NOVEMBER 25TH, 1899

A SPORTSMAN'S NIGHTMARE

TO THE EDITOR OF "COUNTRY LIFE."

SIR,—I send a photograph which I venture to think is at least original. At first sight the sleeping sportsman would appear anxious to rival the Spartan boy of old who hugged a fox to his breast and forbore to cry out, in spite of great inconvenience he is related to have suffered. In this case, however, thanks to the very marked attention his strange bedfellow had previously received from a certain justly celebrated pack of hounds, not to mention subsequent treatment at the hands of the equally celebrated huntsman of the same, the sleeper might have contributed to slumbers indefinitely without suffering any inconvenience, and the spirit of the Spartan boy of old laid to rest on his laurels contentedly in the happy hunting grounds – if he has been lucky enough to get there

"HIS FRIEND SLEPT ON WHOLLY UNCONSCIOUS AND KILLED HIS FOX OVER AGAIN IN HIS DREAMS"

– for the artistic grouping of a mask, brush, hunting crop, hock etc. in and around the couch of the weary Nimrod, is simply the work of the ubiquitous camera fiend who thus took advantage of his friend's fatigue after an extra long hard day. I may add, that so quietly did the friend in question do his work that his friend slept on wholly unconscious and killed his fox over again in his dreams, after a tremendous run; and that's a fact – for I was the dreamer.—J. K. RASHLEIGH

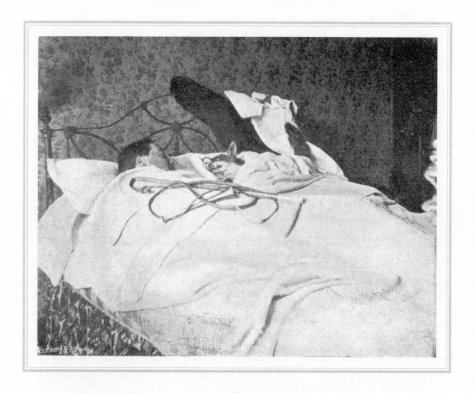

FEBRUARY 4ᵀᴴ, 1899

"ARCADES AMBO"

To the Editor of "Country Life."

Sir,—Herewith I am sending you a couple of recent amateur photographs of my fox-terrier dog, Mr. Jack of Australia, one or both of which I hope you will be able to find a corner for in Country Life. Mr. Jack is ten and a half years of age, and has been my constant comrade since the day of his birth. In his case no teaching of tricks was ever attempted; he takes a pipe in his mouth before the day on which the photograph was taken. To look at him there quietly enjoying himself, it is hard to imagine that he is a terrible fighter, a regular fire eater, bearing numerous honourable scars, all in front. The second photograph shows us enjoying a few minutes' well-earned rest.—E. Mackenzie Maunde-Thompson, South Yarra

JANUARY 27TH, 1900

SPORTING PICTURES ON THE HUMAN SKIN

"**D**ID IT HURT?" was the first question put by an admirer of a very beautiful design done on the arm of a writer by that master of tattooists, Sutherland MacDonald. This very question is one that will be most often heard after an ejaculation of wonderment at the perfection of design which has placed this tattoo artist far above and ahead of any other Western tattooist. It will be well to answer the question at once, "No it does not hurt *much*".

Among Mr. Macdonald's clients there are some of the most distinguished personages of Europe, whilst members of our Royal Family, among them H.R.H. the Duke of York, H.I.M. the Czarevitch, and Imperial and Royal members of Russian, German, and Spanish Courts have also had designs done on their persons by the same artist.

"DID IT HURT?"

Only recently he had a private session which took him to St. Petersburg, while on another occasion he tattooed a millionaire on his yacht whilst enjoying at the time one of the pleasantest yachting trips that has ever fallen to his lot. With some persons the process appears to inflict but very little pain, some having actually fallen asleep during the operation. Personally the writer found no great discomfort in the operation, and the slight soreness caused passed off in a couple of days. In especially sensitive cases a mild solution of cocaine is injected under the skin where the design is to be placed, and no sensation whatever is felt, while the soothing solution is so mild that it has no effect whatever on the person operated upon except locally.

He receives letters from his patrons now in all parts of the world, describing the sensation produced when these skin pictures are seen for the first time. There is such a picture on the back of one of our

Colonial pioneers now in Africa. The superstitious natives regard him with veneration, and imagine his pictures to be infallible proofs of his superiority – in fact, they consider him a demigod – their charm on one occasion helping him out of a difficult and most dangerous situation.— ALBERT H. BROADWELL

THE HAT-TRICK

The true origins of the term 'hat-trick', the feat of taking three wickets in as many balls, are an ongoing source of debate. Country Life *here recounts a few famous hat-tricks of the pre-war days. I Zingari were (and are) the most exclusive of England's wandering cricket clubs.*

IN THE EXHIBITION OF Country Life in Grosvenor Square is a tall white beaver hat. In front of it on the table lies a faded old bow in the red, black and gold of I Zingari. Inside it is the inscription shown in the photograph.

There have been many hat-tricks. The invaluable *Wisden* has a long list of them. Yet, to Cambridge men at any rate, there is only one hat-trick – one that stands infinitely far in front of all the rest: that of the immortal Cobden in the University match of 1870:

> Cobden, whose name in Cambridge Halls,
> The feat unto this day recalls,
> Three wickets with the last three balls,
> To win the match by two.

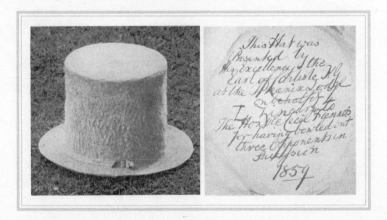

That hat-trick draws me like a loadstone rock and I must come back to it, but meanwhile there is another of an earlier day that ought never to be forgotten. In respect to the quality of the victims, it has some claim to be the greatest of all hat-tricks, and Mr. Altham calls the over in which it was done "perhaps the most famous over in all medieval history." The bowler was the mighty Sam Redgate of Nottinghamshire, as great among the fast round-arm bowlers as Alfred Mynn himself, and he was playing for England against Kent in 1839. The first victim was Fuller Pilch. The match was played for his benefit, and he was entrenched in his own fastness at Town Malling. Redgate was no respecter of persons; he had once before bowled Pitch for a duck in each innings; now, with the first ball of the over he shaved his stumps, and with his second sent them crashing.

"AFTER EACH WICKET FELL, REDGATE DRANK A GLASS OF BRANDY"

The third ball bowled Alfred Mynn; the fourth bowled Stearman, and Stearman, though hardly so famous as the other two, was not a cricketer, as George Brown would say, "for any man to take by the nose." Mr. Pycroft tells, as a legend rather than a historic fact, that after each wicket fell, Redgate drank a glass of brandy. If he really did so, this may partially explain the fact that his career was brilliant but brief.

FEBRUARY 19TH, 1938

A LITTLE ABSTINENCE

THERE CAN SCARCELY be a smoker who has not at some time or other tried to break the chains of his bondage. He may have been ordered to do so (and that, however unpleasant, must make it easier), or he may have suddenly rebelled at the thought of being a slave, and have said defiantly to his pipe: "I'll show you." I myself, though having no reason to think that tobacco harms me, have yet twice abstained for a month at a time; so, at least, I do not write wholly without knowledge. The difficulty is that no one really knows anything on this subject except as regards himself. He who is attempting reform will at one moment be cheered by an already reformed character who declares that after the first few days it does not hurt at all. The next instant he will be utterly cast down by a reprobate who "gave up tobacco for one whole year and found at the end that the longing and the agony were no less than at the beginning."

"AN ADMIRAL MUST *EX OFFICIO* BE AN HONEST MAN"

Either some of these persons are not to be believed, or there is no respect in which human beings more greatly differ. I once sat at dinner next to an Admiral, and an Admiral must *ex officio* be an honest man. He assured me that when he was a young Naval officer he had smoked so much and so regularly that he had seven pipes in commission at once. One day he went ashore without his particular brand of tobacco, whereupon he did not smoke that day, and he never smoked afterwards. I ventured to press him in cross-examination as to whether he really never had tried again, and he admitted that he had once, but found he had altogether lost the taste for it. That is a remarkable story and almost appalling example of resolution and a well regulated mind.

THE BEST MAN

Ah me! that I was thus beguiled,
By one whom I had fondly styled
A friend, – and loved as mine own child,
(That is, till then.)
To be, forsooth, a Wedding Guest,
Nay more, to be myself the "best" –
And I may add, unhappiest, –
Of single men.

Tho' some would count it, I suppose,
Their pride to be so "near the rose,"
But not so I, – I would, Heaven knows,
Much rather not.
I was not born for such delights;
Indeed I cannot sleep o' nights,
For thinking of the awful rites,
The dreadful knot.

And when I think, I have no choice,
But must – officially – rejoice,
(Singing maybe the oft-sung Voice
O'er Eden breathed.)

I feel as sad as any hearse,
My nerves grow daily worse and worse,
I am as one to whom a curse
Had been bequeathed!

—R. D. R.

THE ENGLISH COUNTRY GENTLEMAN

Mr. Arthur Ponsonby, in a book which he has just published and called "The Decline of Aristocracy" – employs a great deal of ingenuity in attempting to find an invidious definition of the word "gentleman." He wanted it as a target for his criticism. The alternative expressions – "aristocrat", "nobility", "upper-class", "society" and "the rich" – are dismissed as not being sufficiently inclusive. He therefore tries to attach a sinister association to the word "gentleman." But in order to do this he has to split a very fine hair.

> "FEW WORDS HAVE COME TO CONVEY SO BEAUTIFUL A MEANING AS THAT OF 'GENTLEMAN'"

The world has given its own meaning to the word "gentleman," and what that meaning is may be inferred from certain well-known phrases. Thus, "Nature's gentleman" by universal consent means a man of humble birth, who, nevertheless, possesses the attributes of courtesy, kindness and consideration for others which are essential to our conception of the perfect "gentleman." In fact, there are very few words which by long usage have come to convey so beautiful a meaning as that of "gentleman." Mr. Ponsonby, therefore, seeks to attach a stigma to the word in its social interpretation; the long and short of it seems to be that he classes as "gentlemen" all those who are or deem themselves enfranchised from the primitive curse of labour. In other words, they have been born "with means enough either to free them entirely from the necessity of having to work, or to adopt a profession merely as a pastime or a temporary occupation."

It would be impossible to deny that there are such idlers in the land; but the latest of the prophets greatly exaggerates their number. His language is the reverse of urbane when he refers to them as "a class that merely vegetates, lives off the fat of the land, and squanders according to their whim and fancy the wealth that others have toiled to create." Suppose that this strong language were to be met, not by a counter-torrent of abuse, but an examination of facts; what would be the result? Is the English country gentleman truly an idler in the land? It is said "by their fruits ye shall know them," and it would be extremely interesting to hear the verdict which some of the critics of the day would have to arrive at if, instead of giving expression to merely personal opinion, they studied the facts of the case. The English country gentleman has from time immemorial been a landowner, and if he were the selfish pleasure-seeking individual that he represented to be, surely that would be reflected in the condition of English land. We believe that many would accept this criterion, because, after looking at a country house, a garden and a park, they conclude that the owner is a mere sybarite who, in Mr. Ponsonby's elegant language, lives off the fat of the land and squanders what others have produced. But is there any other land in the world quite so well cultivated as our English soil? It is very easy to find fault with it, but let a sober comparison be made and England will certainly not come out second best.

FEBRUARY 18ᵀᴴ, 1939

THE PLEASURES OF A COLD

THERE IS AT the moment no subject so eminently topical as that of the common cold. I have got a cold, you have got a cold; all our friends are lapped in bed, and a great sound of snuffling goes up to heaven. "I don't exactly see no good my mindin' on it 'ud do," as Sam Weller remarked when he was wet through in the dickey of the post-chaise. It does as little good as do those rotatory arguments as to whose particular germ we have caught or how we caught it. Let us, then, make the best of a bad cold, and see if there be not some kindly word to be said for it.

> "EVEN IN THE HEAVINESS OF OUR COLD WE ARE CONSCIOUS OF A CERTAIN LIGHTNESS OF HEART"

For its preliminary stages there is surely none. The early throat, which tells us that we have got it and that nothing can ward it off, when cinnamon is in vain and ammoniated quinine a bitter jest, when we rebel against gargling and sniff little tubes under protest – this is pure misery, and ill-tempered misery at that. We have only one hope, that the throat will "melt and resolve itself into dew," and the first cataclysm of sneezes comes as an answer to our prayer. Once that stage is past and the demon of the cold, caged awhile, at last comes out roaring, the worst is really over. Yet, illogically enough, it is at that moment that people begin to be sorry for us and send us to bed. Till our weepings are visible and our trumpetings ring throughout the house, like those of a maddened elephant, we get comparatively little sympathy. We have no evidence but our own statement, and it may even be that on some previous occasion, now uncharitably remembered, our gloomy prophecies have been unfulfilled. Doubtless we ought to have taken to our bed earlier, even at the risk of being deemed imposters, but a certain manly pride – not a wholly despicable quality – prevented us; as it is we are now but shutting the stable door. Nevertheless, there is now a pleasure in bed that we should not earlier have enjoyed. Even in the heaviness of our cold we are conscious of a certain lightness of heart, and we can snuggle with a good conscience. And then there is the lazy ecstasy of reading old books.

I have my own private remedy – it is almost a secret vice – in such cases; I read "Frank Fairlegh, or Scenes from the Life of a Private Pupil." Here also is tushery of a different kind, the duellist Wilford all in black, and Harry Oaklands, with his lip curling in scorn and his hands clenched white with passion, and Cumberland, who instantly proclaims himself an irredeemable villain by brilliant billiards. I am probably flattering myself in the belief that I am the only survivor of an epoch, the only person who still reads "Frank Fairlegh." There are probably others in nooks and corners, but as Mr. Turveydrop remarked, "We are few. I see nothing to succeed us." Yet it is worth having the worst cold that ever reduced a man to a dripping sop to read it yet again.—B. D.

MAY 22ND, 1926

A BACHELOR'S WANTS

To the Editor of "Country Life."

SIR,—Can any of your readers tell me if they know of anything resembling the following idea: A residential bachelors' club where one could have one's own rooms and furniture, but one's meals in the club mess-room; in a good provincial hunting country with stabling or near hunters for hire; nearness to London not a consideration; with a membership of mostly ex-Naval or Army officers; a bit of lawn and garden, if possible, all the better.—BACHELOR

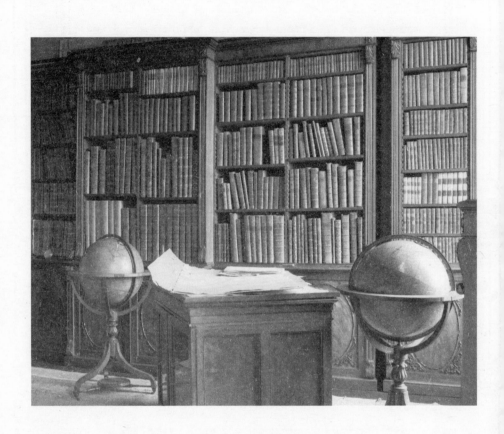

PASTIMES
AND
STUDY

*A gentleman should always have a hobby, even if it is
only the pursuit of idleness.* Country Life *had many
suggestions for how a man could occupy his spare time,
whether in the field, on the water, or among the clouds.*

❖ XII ❖

THE OFFICES OF   LONDON   THE OFFICES OF
"COUNTRY LIFE"   "COUNTRY LIFE"

COLLECTORS' QUESTIONS

*Country Life marshalled experts to answer correspondents' queries on
a vast array of purchases – here is a typically thoughtful and thorough
response to one reader's enquiry of the day.*

I ENCLOSE A photograph of a cricket picture in the M.C.C. collection
in the hope that one of your readers may be able to identify the
locality. The painting is signed W. J. Bowden and dated 1852.
Some of the boundary flags bear the initials L.C.C., and research so far
carried out suggests that the picture might represent the ground of the
Liverpool Cricket Club, then situated at Edge Hill. It seems probable
that the spectators are actual portraits of local patrons of the game.
Unfortunately, nothing appears to be known of the artist, Bowden.—
CURATOR, MARYLEBONE CRICKET CLUB, LORD'S GROUND, LONDON,
N.W.8.

The letters L.C.C., which are said to be decipherable on some of the
boundary flags, narrow the field of enquiry, especially if the date (1852) is
assumed to be correct. The county clubs of Lancashire, Leicestershire
and Lincolnshire had not then been formed, but Liverpool, Lincoln and
other towns had for some years possessed strong clubs of their own. The
suggestion that Liverpool, one of the best known of these clubs, was
perhaps the venue of this match may well be correct, but it would
be difficult now to identify the neighbouring buildings, though the tower
of the church seen on the left of the picture might provide a clue. No
record of a match of such apparent social importance has been traced.
From the excellent quality of the painting one would suppose that the
artist, W. J. Bowden, was of some standing, but there is no mention of
him in any work of reference.

AUGUST 28ᵀᴴ, 1920

A BUTTERFLY HUNT BY THE SEA

BY GEORGE SOUTHCOTE

FOR FULL ENJOYMENT of the cool sea water it is also good to take some exercise first and to get really hot; butterfly-hunting gives an excuse. What is it that teaches butterflies to study effective backgrounds? Why does the Red Admiral spread his black and scarlet beauty on great clumps of yellow fleabane, which blaze in the hot sunshine on the bank bordering the sunny side of the lane? Why does the Peacock, umber red and smoky green, with great black spots dusted with sky blue, poise itself on the right shade of mauve background, provided by the spreading heads of hemp agrimony?

"A WEALTH OF SUNSHINE AND SUMMER SCENES"

We pass through a mysterious shady tunnel where branches of sloe and oak scrub meet overhead, and the sunshine penetrates only in a shimmer of greenish light. Here we find what we are looking for, a pair of Speckled Wood (or Wood Argus) butterflies with their dancing flight, flickering velvety black and lemon yellow in the dim light. A sweep of the net secures them.

An old wooden gate opens on to a wide expanse of luscious green clover, the distant blue sea beyond it far below. The air is heavy with honey-sweet scent from myriads of blossoms, pink and white. The humming of innumerable black and orange bumble bees comes through the gateway with the scent. Many little blue butterflies are flitting from clover head to clover head, and we wait for the chance of the one we want, the smallest of all British butterflies, the wee Bedford Blue, really more brown than blue, but with a bluish gloss to justify its name. Not easy to see, unless you have good sight, and late in the year to find them.

And so to the beach and a glorious swim, followed by the drying of ourselves in the hot sand of a wee valley screened by the dunes. A sleepy revel in the warmth of clothing which we spread in the sunshine to bake while we bathed, and then lazily homewards to set the butterflies and preserve, with them, the memories of a glorious summer's day. Every butterfly in the collection has some association with the surroundings of its capture. A box of them, like the mind of a wise old man, preserves a wealth of sunshine and summer scenes to tide over the cold dark days of winter.

FIG. 1.—Large Blue, Male.

FIG. 2.—Large Blue, Female.

JUNE 2ND, 1928

SHIP MODELS OF NELSON'S DAY

PEOPLE WERE BY no means wanting in the early days of the "boom" in ship models who were ready to predict for it as brief a duration as that which falls to the lot of most collectors' fashions. But time goes on, and, so far, there seems to be no indication of the fulfilment of the prophecy.

The class of model most sought after by collectors at the present time is, undoubtedly, the rigged model of the period somewhat loosely termed "Napoleonic." They are alike desirable from the standpoint of historical and sentimental association and that of aesthetic charm, as well as satisfying the abstract demand of the collector pure and simple for something, whatever it may be, which is the best of its kind.

> "RUSKIN SAID ONCE THAT THE SHIP OF THE LINE WAS ONE OF THE LOVELIEST THINGS EVER CREATED BY MAN"

Ruskin – was it not? – said once that the ship of the line was one of the loveliest things ever created by man. And in Nelson's day that beauty had reached its zenith. Gone was the excess of florid "gingerbread work" which characterised the Navy of the Stuart period, and made the contrast between such ships as the *Prince Royal* and the *Victory* or the *Téméraire* much the same as that between the ormolu-encrusted furniture of the Louis Quatorze school and the severe simplicity of Chippendale, Sheraton and the Adams.—C. FOX SMITH

MARCH 26ᵀᴴ, 1910

THE EXPEDITION OF THE BRITISH ORNITHOLOGISTS' UNION TO THE SNOW MOUNTAINS OF NEW GUINEA

OF LATE YEARS an ever-increasing number of scientific expeditions have been despatched from Great Britain and other countries to investigate the fauna and flora, as well as the geographical features, of unexplored regions of the globe. They have added vastly to our knowledge. Many extraordinary and hitherto unknown forms of animal and vegetable life have been discovered, thanks to the splendid work which has been achieved by enthusiastic travellers and naturalists in all parts of the world. Much, however, still remains to be done, and, outside the Polar circles, few parts are still so little known as the interior of New Guinea or Papua.

The wonderful fauna of New Guinea have long attracted the attention of naturalists in all parts of the world. Until quite recently the hostility of the natives in the southern part of Dutch New Guinea and the risks attending to such an attempt rendered the chances of success too small to justify the experiment, and the Snow Mountains thus remained an unexplored and greatly desired goal for the traveller. The Writer's first intention was to send out a small zoological expedition. However, just at that time (December, 1908) the members of the British Ornithologists' Union, which was founded in 1858, were celebrating their Jubilee, and it seemed fitting that they should mark so memorable an occasion by undertaking some great zoological exploration. The writer therefore laid his scheme before the meeting on December 9th, and his proposal was received with great enthusiasm.

This great undertaking landed at the mouth of the Mimika River on January 5th, 1910. New Guinea must be teeming with unknown wonders, and not the least of these must be the gigantic animal which is reported to inhabit the highlands…—W. R. Ogilvie-Grant

OCTOBER 13TH, 1900

A BILLIARD LOVER

Why should I tremble at your slight,
Or plead my innocence anew?
Lady, I can forget your spite
When from the rack I slip my cue,

And bend above the cloth of green,
Where even you no wrath provoke,
And o'er the rigid cushion lean,
Intent on some strategic stroke.

Lady, how all unworthy you,
Pledged solemnly to be my bride,
These mean remarks about my screw,
These hints, I put on too much side.

Lo, from my soul such dust I flick,
For now my heart with rapture hears
What you may choose to call the click,
But I – the music of the spheres!

My heart with grief shall never fill,
Tho' you with pouting lips should scoff,
And I shall make my cannons still,
Tho' you, exploding, should go off.

My love again you shall not catch
Till in your breast repentance wakes;
Say that you will break off the match –
I but continue making breaks.

Then while I deftly pot the red,
A stroke that Roberts might have missed,
Go, drive suspicion from your head—
Ah ! look, dear Love, the balls have kissed!

—HAROLD BEGBIE

JANUARY 5TH, 1901

A BOOK OF THE DAY

WHEN THE MAN who shoots fares forth on a fine morning in November or December to use his trusty pair of breech-loaders, he expects to have everything, except the act of holding straight, made easy for him. The coverts are, or ought to be, full of birds which have been reared, and fed, and watched the spring and summer through, and he expects that they will be driven over him skilfully and thoroughly. Earlier in the season, or later, he is content to potter about alone and, with spaniel or retriever, to explore the distant spinneys, or the dense outlying hedgerows, and there to pick up a few brace of fine cock pheasants. But this he cannot find time to do in the high-fever days of the shooting season. Now, these things are an allegory.

"THE GAME IS FOUND IN THE BOOKS"

The reviewer is the man who shoots; the pen is his gun; the game is found in the books which, in autumn and early winter, come streaming, not merely in coveys, but in whole packs, from the printing press. The only difference between the reviewer and the shooter is that the latter may use as many cartridges as he pleases, but the former can fire only a limited number of shots. Consequently, the reviewer, in the height of the publishing season, expects to have his books brought up to the gun scientifically and in large numbers, and he simply cannot afford the time

to sally forth and look for books that are not sent, any more than the shooter, at the corresponding time, can go prowling after outlying cocks. Yet these outlying cocks are often the finest birds, and these books which are not brought up to the reviewer are often of the very best quality.

Such is the excuse offered to the reader of COUNTRY LIFE, but not to the publisher of "Peccavi," Mr. E. W. Hornung's latest born and best book, for delay in according to it the appreciative notice which it most unquestionably deserves. To me it was a revelation. Some books written by Mr. Hornung, books written in the dashing and adventurous vein, and concerned often with Australian scenes, I have read with interest and pleasure, but in this book he is on a new and a loftier platform. In it, and against an English background, he deals with a tragic problem, the sin of a man, the ruin and death of a woman, the life-long repentance of the man, and his gradual recovery of self-respect. The result is a book which so enthrals the reader that he simply cannot put it down unfinished.

JULY 24TH, 1937

A CASUAL COMMENTARY: A REFINEMENT OF IDLENESS

I T WILL NOT be very long now before August is upon us, when thousands of houses will be shut, as their occupants start out on their holidays, and a corresponding number of seaside lodging houses will be full. I like to think of all these happy idlers.

I am constantly thinking myself industrious for doing things beforehand, because I cannot bear the thought of having them to do. This is, presumably, better than not doing them at all, but there is not much more to be said for it than that.

Stevenson apologised beautifully for idlers, but his idlers were the genuine article, "cool persons in the meadows by the wayside, lying with a handkerchief over their ears and a glass at their elbow," who watch the busy world go by and refuse to enter for the race. We – the sufferers from my complaint – cannot emulate them, even if we would, and try to look down on them accordingly; but we can hardly conceal from ourselves that ours is but a refinement of idleness. This getting of things done beforehand is a drug, and if taken too freely it saps the manhood. This article is now nearing its close, and for a brief space I may lie with my handkerchief over my ears, but all too soon the image of next week's will loom ahead. And so with those thousands who are now so busily clearing-up. They had better drain that cup to the delicious dregs, for there will be none so sweet when once the holiday has begun. The first week may pass, indeed, with a lovely, gentle, treacherous flow, but after that the game is almost up; when the first half is fled, Black Monday is on us in a flash. Lucky is he who can put off his packing till the cab is at the door. He is the truly sane man, the happy holiday-maker.—B. D.

OCTOBER 18TH, 1902

LARK HUNTING IN WILTSHIRE

A NOTHER RINGING FIGHT now ensues, but again the lark is unable to hold his own in the air long enough to cross the broad valley which lies between us and a thicket of low furze bushes on the crest of the next hill. Long before he is so nearly over this shelter – poor as it is – that he can dive down to it as he did to the oat-sheaves, the Merlin is either already above him or so nearly so that in another half minute she will be able to deliver a stoop which he does not dare to face. Unfortunately, the alternatives are few and almost as risky. Not a hedge nor a ditch, not even a rick or a thick tuft of long grass, is within reach. The only sort of obstacle behind or round which the now desperate fugitive can hope by dodging to puzzle his implacable pursuer is to be found in the bodies of the men who are running so near underneath. Towards one of these accordingly he directs the precipitate course of the fall which he is resolved to take, and, reaching the man – who is still pressing forward, and only half aware of what the lark is doing – some few feet before the foe, swirls round behind him in a sharp curve, thinking thereby to throw out the hawk. Vain fancy! For not for nothing has Keziah so often, when out for exercise, stooped at the soft lure, swung by her trainer with dexterous hand so as to habituate her to seize it even when it is whirled about in the most erratic course. And now, rushing close past the man without alarm or flurry, she strikes the lark full with a whack which sounds almost as loud as that of a racquet against a tennis ball. Her impetus carries her forward, and, gathering up the quarry under her as she flies on, she makes her way with it to the lee side of one of the same stooks in which, in an evil hour, it so artfully hid itself. Here, in due course, she is taken up by her owner; but not in time to save the victim from the swift and sure *coup de grâce*.

> "RUSHING CLOSE PAST THE MAN WITHOUT ALARM OR FLURRY, SHE STRIKES"

JULY 10TH, 1920

LETTERS TO YOUNG SPORTSMEN ON SAILING

BY FRANCIS B. COOKE

Now THAT YOU have your boat you will, of course, be eager to sail her; but, if you are wise, you will curb your desire until you have overhauled the gear and arranged things to your liking. If you do not do this before commencing the season, you will probably never do it at all, and your domestic arrangements will be in a state of chaos all the summer. I should recommend you first to clear out all the lockers so that you may ascertain exactly what there is on board and in what sort of condition it is, and then re-stow the gear in the manner you think most convenient. Every item of the inventory should have its allotted place, and after use should at once be restored to that place. If you make a rule of doing this, you will always be able to put your hand on anything you may want, even in the dark. In most small yachts there is ample locker accommodation for all necessary gear, provided that it is stowed neatly and with method; but you get into the habit of bundling everything into the first locker you come to, you will never be able to find anything.

Until you gain experience you will probably have many an anxious moment when meeting other craft, as you will be in doubt as to whether you will clear her or not if you hold your course. If possible, you should watch closely her relative position with some distant stationary object, say a craft at anchor or a tree ashore. If she seems to be dropping astern, you will, in all probability, pass clear ahead of her, and if she appears to be forging ahead she will pass ahead of you. If, however, she does not seem to move either ahead or astern, you will meet if you both hold your course. Should it be your duty to give way in such circumstances, do it in good time. Just for if you failed to do so you would ram her almost end-on and great damage would result. The prudent thing to do is to luff head to wind, and then, if you touch the other boat, it will be only a sidelong blow and the damage, if any, will be slight.

A GALLEY FOR SMALL CRUISERS.

OCTOBER 7ᵀᴴ, 1899

FERRETING

I T IS RATHER wonderful that a ferret is as amiable as he is. If you or I, good Christian people, were to spend our lives in a box, to leave that box in a stuffy bag, to be let down a rabbit hole for the purpose not of catching the rabbit – that indeed would be a moment perhaps worth the living of all the former life – but of bolting a rabbit, of sending it out for someone else to catch, and then being taken up again directly we came out of the hole and popped back into the bag; under these conditions of life it is conceivable that even a Christian man or woman might sometimes bite. So it is no wonder that ferrets sometimes bite, but rather a wonder that they do not always bite – that they are, in fact, as amiable as they are. To see the rabbit that they have lived up to, so to speak, for weeks and weeks, bolting beyond their ken, without being allowed to go in pursuit, this must indeed be "a sorrow's crown of sorrow" for the poor ferret.

"THERE IS CERTAINLY NOTHING SO CAPRICIOUS AS RABBITS, UNLESS IT BE FISH"

There is a great fascination about this ferreting business – the ferreting, that is, with nets, where the ferreter and the ferret are the sole partners. It is not nearly such good fun bolting rabbits for someone else to shoot, although the shooting is very good fun. Rabbits are the most astonishing little fellows; they have such strange and incomprehensible

FERRETING.

moods. Apparently they get "under the weather" sometimes like trout. There is certainly nothing so capricious as rabbits, unless it be fish. Sometimes they will not bolt, nothing will make them bolt; they will let the ferret scratch nearly all the wool off their bodies, and still they will not bolt. At other times they will start out directly the ferret enters the bury. There seems to be no way of accounting for their quaint caprices. Probably it is some influence connected with the weather or the electricity in the atmosphere, but it is an influence too subtle for the gross human senses to respond to.

DECEMBER 9TH, 1899

YACHTING IN LONDON

For those who didn't have the luxury of sailing the seas, a toy boat on the Thames or the Round Pond in Kensington Gardens was clearly a good alternative.

A FEW WEEKS ago the writer of these lines formed one of a huge crowd on the Thames Embankment. It was damp and chill, a fine mist fell, the roadway was ankle deep in mud, yet thousands of people stood motionless for hours watching two tiny boats moving slowly across a screen. Cold and wet and discomfort were forgotten as they cheered the *Shamrock* when she drew ahead, or groaned as *Columbia* went to the front. Newsboys were shouting "Declaration of war!" England was entering on the greatest fight, the most momentous struggle, of forty years, but the crowd forgot it all for a yacht race. Foreigners came by, shrugged their shoulders, murmured some flattering

allusion to "mad Englishmen," and passed along, not perceiving the real meaning of what they saw, nor understanding that that crowd typified in its own way the impulse of the race.

It is a passion which comes early to maturity. To the small boy, scarcely emancipated from the perambulator, comes the yearning for a boat all his own. And therewith, too, his first lesson in thrift. Aided by a money-box, which no human ingenuity will open, he saves and saves until the day when he too can launch his tiny barque upon the Round Pond. He is at first but a timid mariner, suffering not his precious boat to venture beyond the restraining limits of a cord. But hardihood arrives with age and habit, until at last comes the supreme moment when he trims the sail with unskilful hand and sends forth the tiny craft on her first real voyage. How anxiously he follows her erratic course, trembling when she lies down under a sudden squall, triumphant when her dripping sails emerge from the water, his whole heart going with her as she faces the perils of that great ocean; how eagerly he toddles round to meet her, glowing with all the pride of a great and successful voyage.

"MOST SWIFT AND SHAPELY OF ALL THINGS THAT MOVE WIND-DRIVEN ON THE SEA"

SAND-YACHTING AS
A PAST-TIME

THE IDEA OF utilising the wind to propel vehicles by means of sails on land as well as on sea is probably no new one, but it always means large open spaces and strong winds to obtain good results, and between ice-yachts and land-yachts there is such close resemblance that they might surely be considered first cousins. However, it is only of late years that the sand-yacht has taken practical shape, and sand-yachting is now fast becoming a most popular pastime, and even an interesting sport, wherever long stretches of sand at the seaside give scope to the amateur.

About three years ago M. Louis Blériot, the well-known aviator and designer of monoplanes, was spending a few weeks at Hardelot, the pretty seaside resort on the coast of Picardy, near Boulogne, where, close to his villa, he always keeps a few aeroplanes so as to enjoy flying over the sea on fine days during the summer. The stretch of sand on that coast is marvellous, extending to about eight miles without a break, and at low tide the sea leaves a wide, hard track, smooth enough for any bicycle to ride upon. There also at times the wind blows hard from the sea, and it was no doubt the combination of all these circumstances that gave M. Blériot the idea of constructing his first sand-yacht.

The knack of sailing along by proper handling of the sail is not difficult to acquire, and the steering is most simple. The speed, depending, of course, partly on the strength of the wind and partly on the setting of the sail, can attain twenty miles an hour easily. Watch these two young ladies going along so gaily, and listen to their peals of laughter! Look at the two children who sail in their wake, shouting with delight!

Again, follow further the evolution of the two crafts piloted by the young fellows who, by clever manoeuvring, try to pass each other close to the water, and you will understand why it appeals to so many and to all ages.—NORBERT CHEREAU

OCTOBER 27ᵀᴴ, 1906

THE BOOMERANG, AND HOW TO THROW IT

BY SIR RALPH PAYNE-GALLWEY, BART.

Sir Ralph Payne-Gallwey was a famous shot of his time, as well as being a ballistician and author of several books, including one on the crossbow.

THE BOOMERANG IS a weird and erratic form of missile, and though I have about fifty, and have continually practised with them for many years I have not one that, it may be said, closely resembles another in its behaviour. It is impossible to reproduce with even approximate accuracy a good return in Australian boomerang, owing to the numerous twists and indentations contained in its outlines. These curious twists and hollows represent the experience of generations of native boomerang artists.

All the best Australian boomerangs are closely notched on both surfaces. They are, in fact, roughly honey-combed all over, except on their edges. The Australian gave his Boomerang this rough surface so that it might "bite the air in its flight." For the same reason the outside or cover of a golf ball is indented or pitted, as when golf balls were made with a smooth china-like surface (as was formerly the case) it was found they would not fly far or accurately. There have been many diagrams in various periodicals describing the flight of a boomerang, none of which, in my opinion, has ever clearly indicated its career in the air.

This boomerang evolutionized after several years of modelling, for a chip here, a shaving there, a trifle too little or too much curve, a quarter of an ounce in weight one way or the other or even too thick a coat of varnish, will make or mar one of these fanciful and fascinating playthings. The flight of a boomerang is a scientific puzzle that is never likely to be solved, though many scientists have presented us with learned – though usually divergent – solutions.

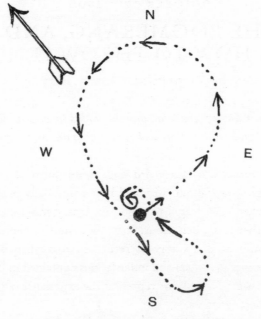

N

W   E

S

*FIG. V.—BIRD'S-EYE VIEW OF THE
FLIGHT OF A BOOMERANG.*

241

Fencing at Westminster School, 1933

Curious Observations

A COUNTRY MISCELLANY

Already Published

'A wonderful reminder of our traditions, our country customs, that it is now, more than ever, important to guard'
JULIAN FELLOWES

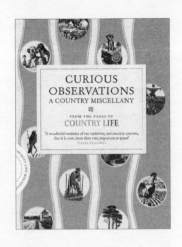

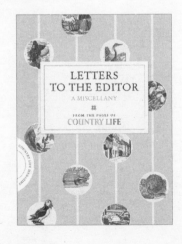

The Glory of the Garden

A HORTICULTURAL CELEBRATION

Already Published

'If you can resist reading these pieces then you are not the sort of person I hope to find myself sitting next to at the dinner table'
ALAN TITCHMARSH

Letters to the Editor

WILL A MEERKAT MAKE
A SUITABLE PET?

October 2012

A 'best of' selection from the thousands of letters COUNTRY LIFE has published in its past. A real treasure trove of the humorous, the splenetic, the joyous and the just plain odd.